101 Great Philosophers

101 Great Philosophers

Madsen Pirie

continuum

Continuum International Publishing Group
The Tower Building   80 Maiden Lane
11 York Road   Suite 704
London SE1 7NX   New York NY 10038

www.continuumbooks.com

British Library Cataloguing-in-Publication Data
A catalogue record for this book is available from the British Library.

ISBN: HB: 978-0-8264-3090-8
      PB: 978-0-8264-2386-3

Library of Congress Cataloguing-in-Publication Data
Pirie, Madsen, 1940-
    101 great philosophers / Madsen Pirie.
      p. cm.
1. Philosophy–History.
2. Philosophers.
I. Title.
ISBN 978-0-8264-3090-8 – ISBN 978-0-8264-2386-3
B72.P49 2009
   190–dc22

                          2009005314

Typeset by YHT Ltd, London
Printed and bound in Great Britain by the MPG Books Group

Contents

Contents

The Ideas of 101 Great Philosophers

This is very much a personal list. It represents the 101 thinkers I have chosen for their impact and significance on human thought. Others might have made a different selection, but almost certainly one with considerable overlap. Anyone familiar with the Western tradition will recognize nearly all the names on this list, and concur with the inclusion of most of them. My list is within the Western tradition of European and American thinkers, and I have taken a broad definition of what it is to be a philosopher.

A few of my choices fall outside the usual modern narrow definition of the word; this is deliberate. Anyone whose thought has changed the way we think about ourselves, our societies or our world, has a potential claim to be included. A handful of scientists, who in previous periods might have been called 'natural philosophers', are included if their work has achieved that.

To feature in this list is in no sense a mark of approval. Some of these thinkers led virtuous lives; others did not. Some have blessed the cause of human happiness; others have blighted it. This book features great thinkers, good and bad, saints and sinners.

Of course, it is not possible in entries as compact as these to give any kind of full account of the contribution each thinker has made. What is presented instead is an introduction to the main ideas of each, to what was original and important about what they said, and perhaps to convey here and there a little of the flavour of their lives. I hope that readers unfamiliar with some of those whose ideas are recorded herein will be tempted to read more of their work, and enter the rich treasure-house of thinking which has been home to our civilization.

1. Thales
c 624–c 547 BC

Thales, from the Ionian city of Miletus in Asia Minor, is hailed as the first philosopher. He speculated about the nature of what he observed, and what reality lay behind appearances. He had travelled to Egypt, acquiring some of their early trigonometry, and could measure the height of a pyramid by the length of its shadow, and estimate the distance of a ship at sea by observations from two points of land.

Thales is said to have predicted the solar eclipse of 585 BC, which event stopped the battle between the Lydians and Medes, persuading them to make peace. He was named as one of the seven sages, with the saying 'Water is best' chosen as his wisest. He was not talking about drink, but about the nature of matter. Thales taught that all things were made of water. He had seen it assume different forms such as ice and mist, and concluded it was the ultimate constituent of matter. He thought the earth itself floated on water, and that earthquakes were caused when it was buffeted by waves.

His ideas may seem simplistic to modern ears, but their importance was that he was seeking natural and comprehensible explanations of things, instead of simply attributing everything to capricious gods. He explored magnetism, noting that some objects could move each other when rubbed and given what we now call an electrostatic charge. He concluded that a magnet must have a soul, classifying it with living things that have the power to move things.

He was versed in mathematics and astronomy, and established that a triangle inscribed within a semicircle must be right-angled and that the constellation Ursa Minor could aid navigation. Thales was the first absent-minded professor, falling into a ditch while looking at stars, prompting a woman to ask how he could possibly know what was happening in the sky if he didn't even know what was at his feet.

Thales was asked why, if he was so clever, was he not rich? His response was to predict from astronomical observations that the next olive harvest would be a bumper one, and to buy futures on olive presses. He leased them out at higher rates when the bumper harvest materialized, simply to show that he could make money if he wished.

He wisely advised people not to do themselves what they would blame in others, and called happy the man who was healthy in body, resourceful in soul, and readily taught.

2. Anaximander
610–546 BC

Anaximander, successor to Thales, has two firsts to his credit, being the first philosopher to write down his ideas, and the first person to draw a map of the world. He lived in Miletus and was regarded highly enough to be appointed leader of its new colony of Apollonia on the Black Sea.

He criticized Thales' idea of water changing into other things, because water cannot contain opposites like wet and dry. Instead, Anaximander sought something more universal, without the characteristics of any one thing. He called it *apeiron*, the unbounded, a substance that is not limited into being any particular thing. It was the original substance from which came both earth and heavens. Everything except *apeiron* is either a source or derived from a source. In its original indeterminate form, there are no opposites because they are all bound together. Only when things separate out into different elements do opposites emerge. Things come from that unbounded substance, and will ultimately return to it. In between those times, opposites encroach on each other, searching to correct the 'injustice' of that initial separation.

Anaximander reasoned that the earth was like a drum, with height one-third of its diameter, and people living on the top surface. This allows for the apparently flat surface we live on, the circular horizon we see, and the fact that heavenly bodies seem to pass beneath it. The earth is unsupported, said Anaximander, because it is at the centre, with no reason to move in any particular direction. He worked out that the sun, moon and stars were at different distances, and thought a great fire was contained in wheels revolving round the earth, and visible through holes in the wheels, whose changing shapes accounted for lunar phases and eclipses.

The earth was once water-covered, thought Anaximander,

but had dried somewhat, and creatures had emerged from the action of sun on wet mud. Humans, frail as they are, must have been protected earlier in their aquatic development, and probably emerged from the mouths of great fish. He thought humans had originally had spines on their skin, as fish do.

In addition to his achievements as a cartographer, Anaximander ventured into meteorology, attributing thunder to the clashing together of clouds. He introduced the gnomon (vertical sundial) into Greece, and used it to determine equinoxes as well as measuring time. As with the other Milesian philosophers, he rejected mythological accounts of events in favour of naturalistic and logical explanations.

3. Pythagoras
c 570–c 490 BC

Known to schoolchildren by the theorem that bears his name, Pythagoras is one of the most influential thinkers who ever lived. Born on the Greek island of Samos, he reputedly visited both Egypt and Babylon before establishing a school in Croton, a Greek city in Italy. His thinking is enmeshed in legends surrounding the man and his followers.

He observed that the musical notes made by plucking a string vary in proportion to its length, just as those made by striking an anvil vary with its size. He deduced that mathematical ratios lay at the heart of musical harmony, and concluded that all reality is based on mathematics. Behind the imperfect world we experience lies the true reality that can be expressed in mathematical formulae. This applies to all objects. The right-angled triangle whose shorter sides measure 3 and 4 has its longest side measuring 5. This was already known to the Babylonians, but Pythagoras proved that the square on the long side of any right-angled triangle equals the sum of the squares of the shorter sides. It is numbers like these, said Pythagoras, that define the shape of the physical object.

Not only did mathematics rule earthly things, Pythagoras taught, but even heavenly bodies moved in the ratio of musical harmonies, making the celestial 'music of the spheres'. Things were part of 'the unbounded' until their shapes and forms were defined by numbers.

Pythagoras thought people were motivated by the pursuit of gain, honour, or wisdom, and to achieve wisdom his adherents led self-disciplined, monastic lives. This involved abstaining from meat and beans, and following strict rituals which included smoothing out the depressions of a pot in the ashes, or of the body in the bedclothes. A balance in life was sought between opposites such as wet and dry or hot and cold. His outlook was a strange combination of the rational and the mystical. His followers lived communally, admitting women as equals, and having property in common.

Pythagoras also believed that living beings had immortal souls which were reincarnated through successive lives. Many of the beliefs passed down in Plato's writings originated first with Pythagoras, including those of a pure reality underlying imperfect appearances; the three drives which motivate people; the reincarnation of the soul; and the merits of a contemplative, simple life.

Pythagoras himself was thought godlike, though it is doubtful that he had the golden thigh which legend attributes to him, or that he was able to project writing on the moon by reflecting it off a mirror.

4. Xenophanes
570–480 BC

Xenophanes of Colophon, who flourished in the fifth century BC, spent his life 'tossed about Greece', as he described his flights from turmoil. He nonetheless lived to old age and left fragments of elegant poetry expressing a philosophy in which his insights can seem remarkably modern.

He was one of the first to reject random acts by gods as the explanation of things, and to seek natural explanations which fitted physical forces to our observations. He founded the Eleatic School of philosophy, whose disciples included Parmenides.

Xenophanes postulated that one supreme god, spherical in shape, eternal and unchanging, and unlike humans in form or nature. Anticipating Feuerbach, he observed that humans equip their gods with human attributes. Ethiopians have them flat-nosed and black, he says, whereas Thracians give theirs blue eyes and red hair. Yet if cattle, horses and lions could draw, their gods would look like themselves.

Furthermore, Xenophanes criticized Homer and Hesiod for encouraging moral degeneracy by describing gods with human weaknesses such as theft, adultery and deceit – incompatible with divine goodness. Writers should tell only creditable stories about gods, he said.

Xenophanes was a social reformer, writing how people should behave at drinking parties, denouncing useless luxuries and decrying the excessive honours bestowed on successful athletes.

Having seen fossils of fish inland, Xenophanes concluded that water had once covered the earth, and that water and earth in various mixtures were the source of all other things. Xenophanes attached particular importance to clouds, seeing them as a transitional phase between one state and another. He thought them 'lifted by the suns rays into the surrounding air', and that the sun consisted of burning clouds, with the moon as a compressed one. He similarly tried to explain other natural phenomena, and thought nature itself to be unlimited, homogenous and eternal, but did not equate it with god.

Human perceptions he regarded as deceptive and subjective: men would think figs sweeter if they lacked honey to contrast them with. Truth exists, but men cannot know it, only speculate about it. By seeking, men can learn things that might resemble the truth, 'but as for certain truth, no man has known it, nor will he know it'. Even if man were by chance to utter the final truth, said Xenophanes, 'he would himself not know it: for all is but a woven web of guesses'. This reflects the modern view of science as a series of hypotheses, none of which can be proved for certain.

5. Heraclitus
c 535–475 BC

Heraclitus of Ephesus was one of the group of Greek philosophers called 'pre-Socratics', not only because they lived and wrote before Socrates but because they wrote about different things from Socrates. Many of them struggled to explain what the universe was all about, why it took different shapes and forms, and whether there was a deeper reality underlying appearances, rather than simply examining human goodness and virtue.

Heraclitus has had a lasting influence. Most of his near contemporaries sought to find the comfort of permanence amid disorder and uncertainty, but Heraclitus embraced change and made it the centrepiece of his philosophy. His work *On Nature* does not survive, but from quotations referred to by other writers, we have a vivid impression of his world view.

Everything, he supposed, is in flux. 'We step and do not step into the same rivers.' His point was that although we call it the same river, new waters have replaced those into which we first stepped. In the world of Heraclitus everything is constantly changing. We are not the people we were before, and the sun is new every day. This opposed the Milesian philosophy which declared that a thing must be what it is, or it doesn't exist at all. Not so, said Heraclitus, because things change over time.

Central to his system is the unity of opposites. 'The way up and the way down are the same,' he tells us, and the same is true of other opposites such as day and night, winter and summer, and war and peace. He does not mean that the opposites are simultaneously identical, but that they are constantly changing into each other. Day replaces night, and night day. Indeed, without day there would be no night. The strife between opposites will never be resolved, and none will ever triumph permanently over its counterpart. The struggle between them is cosmic justice; and all things come through strife.

Heraclitus thought fire to be the primordial element and source of the others – 'all things are an interchange for fire'. Even in men, the most worthy souls were dominated by fire, and less contaminated by 'base' water. War, the embodiment of strife, was embraced by Heraclitus as 'father and king', deciding the status of men.

He had no time for conventional politics, declaring his fellow-countrymen 'should be hanged', and preferring games with children to public life. He refused favours from the Persian king because he disliked luxury. Perhaps because of these traits he was long regarded as an archetype of melancholy.

6. Parmenides
   ## c 515–450 BC

Little is known of the life of Parmenides, but it is recorded that in his 65th year he met and influenced the youthful Socrates. Of his influence on the world of ideas there can be no doubt. He was the first in a long tradition of philosophers who used arguments based on logic and language to deduce things about the outside world, deductions which do not rely on observation and in many cases run counter to it.

Parmenides wrote in hexameter verse, of which only about 150 lines survive out of many more. His work *On Nature* tells how he was transported in a chariot by a goddess through 'the gate of night and day'. She showed him the difference between 'the way of truth' and 'the way of opinion', and Parmenides gives us the arguments that support this division.

For us to be able to think and talk about something, it must 'exist', he says, for we cannot think about that which is not. When we think about things in the past they must still exist as they were then, and for us to be able to think about things in the future they must exist now. So Parmenides deduces that change is illusory; things continue to exist as they eternally are.

Furthermore, 'that which is' could not have come into being, for 'nothing comes from nothing'. Reality is thus, according to Parmenides, eternal and unchanging. Furthermore, it is uniform. Since motion is illusory because there can be no nothingness between objects, the universe must be the same throughout. It is an indivisible, static sphere, he tells us.

Countering Heraclitus' claim that all is change, Parmenides sets the opposite view of a more reassuring permanence in which *nothing* changes. The universe, he says, is a single entity which always was, always will be, and is the same throughout. Observation does not show us this because the senses belong to the world of opinion rather than that of truth. Only pure reason (or 'logos') can show us truth.

Parmenides concludes that the universe is substance, rather than process. Its form may appear to change as objects are made and destroyed, but the material they are made from endures eternally, and its different appearances are only part of that illusory 'world of opinion'.

Parmenides' argument depends on words having a constant, fixed meaning, but people do not use words in that way. Their meaning changes over time, and few people now suppose that words alone can endow objects with immortality.

7. Anaxagoras
c 500–428 BC

Born in Ionia in modern Turkey, Anaxagoras spent 30 years in Athens initiating its tradition of philosophical and scientific speculation. He befriended and influenced the statesman Pericles and the playwright Euripides, and produced a totally materialistic account of the cosmos which led to his prosecution and conviction for impiety. Pericles intervened and Anaxagoras escaped punishment by exile.

His fame rests on his interpretation of the material world, his cosmology, and his use of mind ('nous') as the driving force in the universe. He sought to reconcile the view of Parmenides that things could not come into existence or pass away with the visible evidence of change in the sensory world. He concluded that 'everything contains a portion of everything else', and that the food which changes into flesh and bone does so because it already contains those things. 'For how can hair come from not hair,' he asks, 'or flesh from not flesh?' All things are made up of small parts of everything else, but there is no smallest particle, or it would be only one thing. Particles must be infinitely divisible, he concluded, with no smallest and no largest. The constituent predominant in things is what makes them what they are.

The universe began with everything packed together in one mass. It was set spinning by 'nous', and became a vortex, like those on earth, but larger. It separated into two great masses, the outer one hot, dry ether, and the inner one of moist air. The latter developed first mist, then water, earth and stones, progressively colder at each stage. The earth, flat in shape, was supported by its size and by the air it rested on.

Anaxagoras thought the sun was a red hot stone in the sky, while the moon shines by its reflected light. He correctly accounted for solar eclipses by the moon blocking its light, and lunar eclipses by the blocking of its sunlight. The moon was made of earth, he said, with plains and valleys on it, and meteorites are stones shaken free of the heavenly vortex.

The 'nous' which set this going is different from everything else, and does not contain portions of them. It is 'the finest of all things and the purest'. Nowhere, to the displeasure of Socrates and Aristotle, does Anaxagoras attribute purpose behind his system; it operates mechanically.

In addition to his ideas, Anaxagoras bequeaths his spirit of enquiry. Asked the point of being born, he replied, 'to study the universe'.

8. Empedocles
c 492–c 432 BC

Although he wrote two and a half millennia ago, Empedocles is surprisingly modern in some ways. A Greek native of Sicily, he was one of the first who did not take the world around him for granted, but wondered why things were as they were and how they change. He wondered how life had begun, and what happens after death.

He wrote in verse, many fragments of which survive. His works *On Nature* and *Purifications* might be separate, or perhaps parts of one larger work. It is to Empedocles that we owe the ancient division of things into their constituent parts. He thought that all things were made up of four basic building blocks which others would call elements, and that these were earth, air, fire and water. They combined into different mixtures and arrangements to make up different objects.

Empedocles even supplied a mechanism in the shape of two forces: Love and Strife. They struggled against each other, alternately gaining the upper hand. We might think of them as attraction and repulsion. It all started, Empedocles said, with a sphere united by 'Love' in which the four constituents were together but unmixed. They separated into the different forms of matter, combining in different proportions.

As for living things, they started with body parts combined in fantastic combinations, with only those able to survive managing to endure. This was not Darwin's theory of evolution, any more than his original sphere was the primeval atom, but his account is a startling precursor of modern thought.

Empedocles ingeniously accounted for our sensation of things. Invisible particles from objects impinge on our sense organs and our pores, and are detected by similar particles there. He even suggested that the moon shines by reflected light, and that light takes time to cross the space between objects. Again, the ideas strike us as quite modern in their approach. He tried to account for the different forms of matter, how they change over time, and how we interact with them.

Contemporaries regarded him as something of a magician, attributing healing powers and the ability to control weather. He praised vegetarianism and believed in reincarnation. Empedocles seems to have claimed some god-like powers; he did think he was immortal, and is reputed to have jumped into Mount Etna to prove it. He failed, leaving Bertrand Russell to quote an unnamed poet, 'Great Empedocles, that ardent soul, Leapt into Etna and was roasted whole.'

9. Protagoras
c 490–420 BC

Protagoras is hailed as the greatest of the sophists – scholars who earned their living by teaching rhetoric, a prerequisite for public life in ancient Athens. Protagoras also taught analysis of poetry, and was the first to systematize grammar and syntax, which he also taught. He claimed he could teach virtue, too; a claim featured in Plato's dialogue *Protagoras.* He befriended Pericles, and wrote the constitution and laws for the Athenian colony of Thurii in Italy.

Of surviving fragments, his most famous quotation is that 'Man is the measure of all things – of what is, that it is, and of what is not, that it is not.' This marks out his relativism, the belief that there are no objective and eternal standards, but that they vary with the individual. Only a person can judge whether they feel hot or cold, and different people experience things differently. Protagoras thought that beauty also was relative, and more controversially that this applied in such areas as virtue, truth and justice. What is true for one person might be false for another, he taught, because there is no objective truth. Our interpretation of the world is necessarily subjective, he taught, and nothing is inherently good in itself.

Although Protagoras was reportedly honest and polite himself, some of his students were less scrupulous, using clever arguments to win unjust cases and bringing the word 'sophist' towards its modern meaning denoting unethical cleverness. Protagoras was blamed by some because he had taught 'how to make the worse case appear better', and he was pilloried by the comic poet Aristophanes in *The Clouds.*

Protagoras may be the first recorded agnostic. He wrote: 'Concerning the gods, I have no means of knowing whether they exist or not or of what sort they may be.' 'Many things prevent knowledge,' he said, 'including the obscurity of the subject and the brevity of human life.' Protagoras began the move which turned philosophical attention away from the universe and into the study of human values. His relativism and his lack of any divinely set standard led later thinkers, starting with Plato, to seek the permanence of transcendental and eternal truths about justice, virtue, and the nature of human experience.

Protagoras held views on punishment, reports Plato, that were enlightened for his era. It was that its purpose was to deter the culprit from repeat offences, rather than to exact society's revenge. It fits with the accounts of him as a sensible and thoughtful man.

10. Zeno
c 490–430 BC

Zeno of Elea is remarkable for negative, rather than positive, contributions to philosophy. A disciple of Parmenides, he supported his mentor's view of a single, indivisible universe by eliciting the absurdities of the contrary view. He denied the existence of different things, or of real motion, by showing the inconsistencies and impossibilities this entailed. He did this through a series of paradoxes which even today can engage and intrigue.

Zeno visited Athens with his master when he was about 40 and Parmenides 65. They talked with the young Socrates, a discussion preserved in Plato's dialogue *Parmenides.* Aristotle credits Zeno with the invention of dialectic, the method of trying to bring out inconsistencies through dialogue with an opponent. Zeno did introduce the *reductio ad absurdum,* still in use, which shows a position to be untenable because of the absurdities it leads to. Some credit him with the start of modern logic.

Zeno may have identified 40 paradoxes, of which few survive. The most famous concerns Achilles and the tortoise. Achilles, chasing the tortoise at ten times its speed, starts 100 feet behind it. When he has covered that distance the tortoise has gone ten feet. Each time that Achilles covers the gap, the tortoise has gone one tenth ahead, so Achilles never catches the tortoise even though he is ten times as fast. The paradox occurs by choosing shorter and shorter distances, always short of the overtaking point.

Also celebrated is the racecourse paradox. To cross it, you first must cross half of it. And before that, you need to cross half of that half. Before every fraction you must first cross half of it, and with infinite subdivision, you never manage to cross.

Because at any instant in an arrow's flight, it occupies a fraction of space, it is at rest for that instant, said Zeno. Given an infinite number of such spaces, the arrow in flight is always at rest.

He wanted to demonstrate the impossibility of infinite subdivision of distances and times, showing that our sensory experience of different objects and of motion must be deceptive. These are more than clever tricks, for they reach to the heart of how our minds can conceive space, velocity and time intervals. They are no longer paradoxes to modern scholars, but they did inspire Greek thinkers to seek physical accounts of matter, rather than proposing mixtures of different things. And they persuaded Democritus and the atomists to propose tiny indivisible constituents of matter.

11. Diogenes
c 472–323 BC

There are no surviving writings by Diogenes of Sinope, dubbed 'the Cynic', but we have a vivid picture of the man and his ideas from those who wrote about him. Diogenes was not a cynic in the modern sense of questioning people's motives. In his case, the description came from the Greek *knyikos*, or dog-like, because he was thought to live like a dog.

It was said that the oracle at Delphi told him to 'debase coinage', which was remarkable since his father was implicated in a real debasing of coinage at Sinope and Diogenes had been exiled with him. However, Diogenes took the Delphic utterance to mean that he was to debase the coinage of custom, and went to Athens to do so.

Humans live artificially, taught Diogenes, repressed by civilization. A dog, by contrast, eats when hungry and performs bodily functions unashamedly in public. Diogenes became notorious for his eccentric lifestyle, which included a dog-like carelessness of manners and decency as he flouted convention. Plato said he was 'like Socrates gone mad'. He wore rough clothes, ate plain food, and eschewed any kind of luxury. Indeed, he scorned it, along with the vanity and hypocrisy of civilized life. He lived in a tub, having no need of a house, and when he saw a boy drinking water from cupped hands, he threw away his wooden bowl as an unnecessary luxury.

He used wit and intelligence to mock the fashionable sophisms of other philosophers. Having heard Plato's definition of a man as a featherless biped, Diogenes plucked a chicken and presented it to Plato's class as an example of a man. Plato subsequently added 'having broad nails' to his definition.

Diogenes was reportedly seized by pirates on a journey and sold as a slave in Corinth. When asked what skills he had, he replied 'governing men', and asked to be sold to someone who needed to be governed. He was sold to Xeniades to tutor his sons.

When Alexander the Great visited him at Corinth, he found Diogenes sunning himself and asked if there were anything he, Alexander the Great, could do for him. Diogenes replied that he could stand out of the sunlight, and Alexander is alleged to have said that if he were not Alexander, he'd rather be Diogenes.

Diogenes claimed that 'to fortune he could oppose courage, to convention nature, to passion reason', and his indifference to life's comforts powerfully influenced later philosophers, including the Stoic school.

12. Socrates
c 469–399 BC

Socrates is a pivotal figure in Western philosophy, partly for his philosophical approach and method, and partly because his life is regarded as a model and inspiration. Greek philosophers are divided into pre- and post-Socratic. He nonetheless remains an enigma because he wrote nothing himself, leaving our knowledge of the man and his ideas to accounts by others. Plato in particular used dialogues featuring Socrates to illustrate philosophical ideas, but much of what is said clearly represents Plato's own later development rather than his mentor's thinking.

Socrates was reportedly quite ugly, with bulging eyes and a flat, flared nose, and went around barefoot and unwashed. In *The Clouds* by Aristophanes there is a comic portrayal of him teaching youths to evade debts.

He had been a stonemason, but gave it up to teach philosophy, charging no fees. He was to be found at the marketplace, engaging people in dialectical enquiry, the so-called 'Socratic Method'. The oracle at Delphi described him as the wisest man, and a surprised Socrates set out to question supposedly wise people, cross-examining them about their knowledge. Discovering this was scant, he understood that his wisdom lay in alone knowing his ignorance.

The Socratic Method questions what people think they know, trying to elicit internal contradictions so that the initial assertion is rejected for more consistent hypotheses. Socrates used it destructively to show that conventional ideas about such things as love, honour, virtue and courage were inadequate. In doing so, he irritated important people by making them seem ill-informed.

To Socrates wrong-doing comes from ignorance, not deliberate evil, whereas wisdom leads to virtue, and life should be spent searching for the good. He advocated a simple life, a theme that later inspired both Cynicism and Stoicism.

Following political turbulence in Athens, Socrates was charged with corrupting youth and promoting impiety. In fact he seems to have observed religious ritual, and claimed an 'inner voice' alerted him if he were about to do wrong.

Socrates' students included rich young men scornful of democracy, some of whom had participated in the rule of the Thirty Tyrants which briefly overthrew it. In Plato's *Apology* we hear his defence, that he opposed ignorance and sought good, and in Plato's *Phaedo* we read how he accepted the court's death sentence, unafraid of death, and obedient to the laws he had accepted. He drank the hemlock and passed into legend, 'the finest man of his generation, the wisest, too, and the most righteous'.

13. Democritus
c 460–370 BC

Democritus was called the 'laughing philosopher' because of his cheerful temperament, and because the absurdity of human follies amused him. He is more widely known for the atomic theory of matter. A pupil of Leucippus, some of whose ideas he elaborated and systematized, Democritus had travelled to Egypt and Babylon, and perhaps to India, picking up some of the knowledge of different countries. He discovered that a cone has a third of the volume of the cylinder of the same base and height, and is reported to have known about herb extracts and their properties. His writings are recorded only in fragments quoted by other writers.

He tried to reconcile conflicting ideas about reality. Parmenides had said that nothing can come from nothing, and that nothing changes. Heraclitus had pointed to the constancy of change. In a stunning *tour de raison*, Democritus postulated that the universe consists of two things: atoms and the void. Atoms are the tiny indivisible particles which make up everything. They are eternal, incompressible, and in motion. The void is not 'nothingness', but space through which atoms can move. The collisions and assemblies of atoms account for the different things we perceive. These are not eternal because their atoms can form new associations; but the atoms themselves are indestructible.

Democritus said that atoms vary in shape and size, and in their surfaces. Some have fine hooks and can easily attach with others in clusters to form solid objects; others are smoother, associate less readily, and form looser materials such as water. When we sense things, it is because the atoms of objects are interacting with the atoms in our eyes, nose, ears, tongue and hands. This means that senses are deceptive. Properties like sweet and bitter are not in the atoms themselves. 'By convention hot, by convention cold, but in reality atoms and void, and also in reality we know nothing, since the truth is at bottom.'

The account Democritus gives is entirely mechanistic; there is no purpose or direction in his universe, which has always existed. He thought gods were used by the populace to account for the seemingly inexplicable. Our souls, he said, are made of very fine atoms forever in motion, like those of fire, and they move our bodies.

His ethical stance urged pleasure, which he thought 'the distinguishing mark of things beneficial', but in moderation, which he thought enhanced it. His advocacy of a tranquil life undisturbed by fear or superstition greatly influenced his successors.

14. Antisthenes
c 446–366 BC

A student of Socrates and teacher of Diogenes, Antisthenes was a bridge between the Socratic ethical life and its more robust expression in the Cynic philosophy of Diogenes. Antisthenes, having learned rhetoric under Gorgias, switched to Socrates, encouraging other students to do likewise. Antisthenes flaunted his rejection of material pleasures with his untidy dress and unkempt beard. Socrates, noting how the holes in his threadbare cloak were visible, not hidden, remarked, 'I see your vanity through the holes in your cloak.'

Antisthenes went beyond Socrates' teaching. He equated happiness with virtue: the happy man was the virtuous one. Furthermore, virtue could be taught, and once acquired, never lost. Antisthenes taught people to shun external things like property and pleasures, and instead pursue inner things such as truth and self-knowledge. The simple, ascetic life was the path to wisdom and virtue, whereas the pursuit of pleasure led to reckless and foolish behaviour. Desire enslaved people, and to say 'May the sons of your enemies live in luxury' was to curse them.

Antisthenes wrote over 60 books, most of which are lost. His concern was ethics and virtue sought through simplicity, and it was behaviour that mattered, not theory. He carried a beggar's knapsack and staff, and while people disdained his poverty, he himself disdained esteem, calling ill-repute a blessing. He brought a caustic sense of humour to his teaching, once urging the Athenian assembly, which voted to make people generals, also to vote to make asses into horses. It was better, he said, to fall among crows than among flatterers (a pun in Greek) because the ones devour only the dead whereas the others devour the living.

Socrates had taught obedience to society's laws, but Antisthenes urged his followers to pursue virtue even when it conflicted with law. His ethics lacked religious backing, for he said there were no universal truths. He thought there was a single god in nature, but not one that resembled anything on earth, and not one that Antisthenes regarded with any religious feeling. Cicero later complained that this deprived divinity of all meaning and substance.

Antisthenes admired Heracles for his virtue and valour, and urged his followers to develop stamina as well as virtue. He was a competent wrestler himself, and had distinguished himself by bravery at the battle of Tanagra. But it was his concern with cultivating wisdom and virtue which set him among those who turned philosophy inward to the self rather than outward to the world.

15. Plato
427–347 BC

Plato, one of the most influential classical philosophers, wrote in an entertaining, accessible style. Most of his works are cast as dialogues, conversations between his mentor, Socrates, and others. Plato is not a character in these dialogues, so many assume that Socrates expresses Plato's views.

In these discussions, Plato explores the meaning of things like justice and love, and examines what constitutes a balanced life or a just state. Typically, Socrates cross-examines his interlocutors to clarify the essentials of the point at issue, and Plato's philosophy emerges from the collection of such dialogues.

Plato believed that earthly objects are but pale shadows, or representatives, of their ideal, perfect forms, and that the philosopher should try to gain insights to that perfection. He likened our view to prisoners in a cave watching shadows of things cast on a wall by the light of a fire, and only dimly able to appreciate what the reality might be like. By living a just and contemplative life, the philosopher might gain some sense of those perfect forms.

Plato said the soul consists of three elements: the appetitive, which seeks satisfaction of basic desires; the spirited, represented by qualities such as courage; and a third part belonging to the mind, the intellectual side. A balanced mind keeps the three elements within their proper domain, not allowing any to rule unduly.

In his *Republic*, Plato says these three parts of the soul correspond to the three classes in society. There are the rulers, the soldiers and the common people, and they can be likened to the metals gold, silver and bronze in their qualities and worth. A just state, like a just mind, will have each keep to its own appropriate domain. We can secure just rulers, said Plato, by training them to shun worldly temptations.

To apply his ideas, Plato twice sailed from Athens to Syracuse to advise the tyrants Dionysius and Dion on good government, but both trips ended ignominiously. More lastingly, Plato founded the Academy, a school for philosophers. Plato believed in reincarnation, and that people could live many successive lives before achieving the eternal peace and bliss gained by a philosophical life. He said that knowledge was recollected from previous lives rather than learned, and in one dialogue, *Meno*, elicits the memory of geometry from an untutored slave.

In his *Symposium*, Plato puts the case for a love separated from physical fulfilment ('Platonic' love), yet another aspect of the detached philosophical life he advocated.

16. Aristotle
384–322 BC

Aristotle and Plato were the most influential philosophers of the ancient world; Aristotle more so because he covered more subjects. His thinking provided the foundation of European intellectual development, together with the systems which dominated thought for two millennia.

He joined Plato's academy at 17 and rapidly became a teacher of rhetoric and dialectic. When Plato died, Aristotle went to Assos and did the research on biology which formed the basis of the science, and thence to Philip's court in Macedonia, where he tutored the young Alexander the Great. Returning to Athens with Alexander's backing, he founded the Lyceum to rival the Academy, teaching more subjects.

It is from lecture notes never intended for publication that his ideas endure. He wrote on physics, metaphysics, biology, logic, meteorology, astronomy, psychology, literary analysis, ethics and politics, often pioneering the whole discipline.

His logical treatises set out universal rules of reasoning, including inductive and deductive inferences and syllogistic reasoning. Aristotle's classic syllogism, still used, is of the form 'All men are mortal; Socrates is a man; therefore Socrates is mortal.'

In metaphysics, Aristotle explores the fundamental principles of existence. He examines the essence of things, determining that they have 'substance', made up of matter and form; a notion carried through into mediaeval scholasticism. He identifies four causes of everything: the material cause it is made of; the formal cause which is what it is; the efficient cause which is the means of its creation; and the final cause which is its purpose.

Writing on ethics, Aristotle observes that everyone seeks happiness, but having life's necessities is insufficient. Wise people seek true happiness through moderation, for every virtue lies between two extremes of vice, at the 'golden mean'.

'Man,' says Aristotle, 'is a political animal,' and his natural home is a self-sufficient city state. This derives from the natural relationships of man and wife (for procreation), and between master and slave (for mutual survival). Aristotle asks who rules a state, and in whose interest is it ruled? He identifies monarchy, aristocracy and 'polity' ruling for the general good, with their self-serving 'deviations' into tyranny, oligarchy and democracy. He praises 'polity' (rule by moderate wealth) for its stability.

Aristotle's universe is concentric. It has five elements, starting with earth at the centre. Then come water, air and fire, and finally, ether, the stuff of the heavens. This geocentric model, along with Aristotle's other ideas, was later treated as the absolute truth, something never claimed by Aristotle himself.

17. Epicurus
341–270 BC

Epicurus corresponds to the popular impression of a philosopher who teaches us how to moderate our desires and attain tranquility. As with Stoicism and cynicism, the word epicurean diverges today from the philosophy it once represented. An epicurean today describes someone who appreciates sensual pleasures, especially fine food, but that is not what Epicurus taught.

He taught that the highest good is happiness, best attained by avoiding pain and fear, and by being satisfied with modest rather than extreme pleasures. Although only fragments survive, we know much about Epicurus from other philosophers, notably his Roman follower Lucretius who wrote a systematic account in *The Nature of the Universe*.

At his Athens school called 'the Garden', which was indeed in a garden, Epicurus taught that events are caused by atoms colliding in a void. He added to the atomic theory of Democritus the twist that atoms can swerve for unpredictable reasons, allowing Epicurus to reject a deterministic system. There is no purpose or plan behind the collision of atoms. He was thoroughly empiricist as well as mechanistic, telling his followers to believe only what derived from observations and deductions made about them.

The gods, he said, are immortal and blessed, but do not interact with humans at all, giving people no reason to fear them. Nor should humans fear death either, for since it meant the end of consciousness and sensation, it could bring no suffering. In life, good and bad are defined by the pain and pleasure they bring, and one should let the likely balance of them direct ones actions. Overindulgence is likely to lead to pain, whereas a state of modest satisfaction and tranquility will yield a greater balance of happiness.

Epicurus elevated friendship as one of life's greatest pleasures, and praised the satisfaction of 'natural' desires for food and shelter, over the 'vain' desires for power and wealth. Anxiety and fear were great sources of pain and unhappiness, especially fear of death or divine punishment, he taught, whereas in fact earthquakes and natural disasters were caused by the movement of atoms rather than the wrath of the gods. His disciples shunned politics on the grounds that it led ultimately to pain.

The philosophy of Epicurus offered a life-affirming and practical guide, which might account for its enduring appeal. Over the gate of his 'garden' school was written, 'Stranger, here you will do well to tarry; here our highest good is pleasure,' and Epicurus taught that pleasure went with wisdom and justice.

18. Aristarchus
   ## c 310–230 BC

Aristarchus of Samos was a mathematician and astronomer whose calculations led him to suppose that the earth people inhabit is a very small part of a gigantic cosmos, and that it revolves around the sun. He preceded Archimedes, who wrote about his later views, and we have a record of his early work *On the Sizes and Distances of the Sun and the Moon.*

Initially taking the prevailing geocentic view, Aristarchus reasoned that since the moon shines by reflected light, at half-moon it must be at right angles to the sun from the earth. He was thus able to draw its position on a triangle and calculate the ratio between the sides. He concluded that the earth was 18 times farther away from the sun than from the moon (the actual ratio is about 400 times – Aristarchus' method was sound, but he lacked accurate instruments with which to measure).

Knowing from eclipses that the sun and moon were the same apparent size from the earth, and having an estimate of their respective distances, he calculated that the sun's radius must be 30 times larger than the moon, and 7 times larger than the earth. With an estimate that the sun's volume was 300 times that of the earth, and reckoning that smaller bodies revolved around larger ones, Aristarchus at some stage switched to the view that the earth described a circular orbit around the much larger sun.

Archimedes, a younger contemporary, wrote to King Gelon that Aristarchus of Samos held the view that 'the universe is many times larger than generally assumed by astronomers, and the fixed stars are at an enormous distance from the sun and planets'. Because there was no measurable parallax, Aristarchus took the fixed stars to be at a near infinite distance from earth. He took the sun to be one of the fixed stars, but much nearer to the earth than the others.

Aristarchus thus held a view of the earth as a tiny speck in a gigantic universe, a view which diverged from contemporary opinion, and which upset religious convention. Cleanthes the Stoic wrote *Against Aristarchus*, calling for his prosecution for his 'impiety for putting in motion the hearth of the universe', while Dericyllides declared that he 'set in motion the things which by their nature and position are unmoved, such a supposition being contrary to the theories of mathematicians'.

Aristarchus apparently escaped prosecution, and is now regarded as one of the most far-sighted thinkers of the classical era.

19. Archimedes
c 287–212 BC

Archimedes of Syracuse, one of the greatest mathematicians who ever lived, had a profound impact in several areas of study. In addition to studies in physics and astronomy as well as mathematics, he engaged in practical engineering and developed several useful inventions.

Archimedes used knowledge and intellectual skill not just to understand the world, but to change it. The devices he constructed enabled people to achieve what would have been impossible without them. The water-screw he developed had a spiral rotating in a cylinder to lift water from a lower to a higher level. Originally designed to pump water out of ships, it had applications in irrigation.

His most famous discovery was 'Archimedes' principle'. Tasked with finding if King Hieron's golden laurel crown had been diluted with silver, Archimedes realized, allegedly in his bath, that bodies displace their own volume of fluid. Establishing the volume of the crown enabled its density, and therefore purity, to be calculated from its weight. The story is that Archimedes ran out naked shouting 'Eureka!' – I've found it!

He established the principle of the lever, realizing that a great weight at a small distance could be balanced by a small weight at a large distance, and constructed devices to move ships. 'Give me a lever long enough and a place to stand, and I will move the earth,' was his reported claim. He similarly developed a pulley system that would lift heavy objects. He is credited with many more inventions, including a model planetarium.

Archimedes disdained these activities, esteeming mathematics as pure speculation 'without the vulgar needs of life'. He anticipated integral calculus with his 'method of exhaustion', using 'infinitesimals' to calculate areas and volumes. Measuring the areas of a circle as pi times its radius squared, he calculated a value of pi still used as an approximation. He calculated square roots, and even estimated the number of grains of sand in the universe using a heliocentric model of it. His finest achievement, he thought, was to calculate that a sphere circumscribed by a cylinder has two-thirds of the cylinder's area and volume (including the ends).

He developed war machines in the ultimately unsuccessful defence of Syracuse against a Roman siege, but was killed by a Roman soldier when he declared himself too preoccupied with a problem to meet the conquering general Marcellus. His influence reverberated with Arab mathematicians, the Renaissance, and Galileo, and he moved the earth not with a lever but with his ideas.

20. Seneca
c 4 BC–AD 65

Seneca (the Younger) was by some accounts less admirable than his philosophy. A Roman Stoic philosopher, he taught self-discipline and the virtues of a simple life with modest desires, while living somewhat differently himself. Born in Roman Spain of wealthy and well-connected parents, he went to Rome and achieved fame as a writer, a philosopher and a politician. It was during his seven-year banishment to Corsica by Caligula for adultery with the emperor's sister that he wrote many of the works on which his reputation rests. He wrote plays, essays and letters, chief among which are his *Consolations* and his *Moral Epistles to Lucilius*.

Rather than set out a systematic account of the Stoic philosophy he espoused, Seneca wrote letters of comfort and consolation, and advice on how one should behave. His was thus a very practical philosophy, setting out lessons for everyday life about how to achieve virtue. His letters are full of insights on appropriate behaviour.

Recalled from exile under Claudius to tutor the emperor's stepson, Nero, Seneca became Nero's adviser when the latter became emperor, and won praise for the promising early years of that reign, reportedly becoming a wealthy man in the process.

Central to his philosophy was the importance of self-control. 'No man is great or powerful,' he wrote, 'who is not master of himself.' People should train themselves every day to moderate their desires: 'We should every night call ourselves to an account: what infirmity have I mastered today? what passions opposed? what temptation resisted? what virtue acquired?' People should also seek each opportunity to do a kindness to others.'

They should accept suffering because it improves them. He wrote that 'fire tests gold; adversity tests strong men'. Above all, people should accept that there is nothing in death itself as terrible as the fear of it. The true Stoic, said Seneca, will try to live not ruled by emotions, but by rational responses. Anger was especially to be avoided, as were fear and grief. He likened enthrallment by such emotions to actual slavery. Instead, a person should learn to moderate their responses to fortune, and to bear unhappiness with courage. He consoles those in adversity by showing how reason can help them master their grief.

Seneca faced his own death bravely enough. Implicated in a plot against the now depraved Nero and ordered to commit suicide, he opened his veins, took poison, and finally jumped into a hot bath, suffocating in the steam.

21. Epictetus
AD 55–135

Like some other Stoic philosophers, Epictetus appears an attractive and admirable figure to modern eyes, teaching and practising a degree of self-discipline attainable by few. Born a slave in Hieropolis, he was taken to Rome and studied under the Stoic Musonius Rufus. He was lame, possibly injured by his master. He gained his freedom, but was exiled, along with other philosophers, by the Emperor Domitian, choosing to settle and teach philosophy at Nicopolis in Greece, and drawing widespread recognition and acclaim.

Neither of his two works was written by himself, but by his student, the historian Arrian, who used to write down what Epictetus said. The *Discourses* provide guidance for the philosophical life, covering such topics as composure, friendship, and coping with illness. The *Handbook* encapsulates the basic Stoic themes, supported by lively anecdotes.

The purpose of philosophy, Epictetus teaches, is to enable us to live better lives, to achieve happiness. It begins with self-examination. We must divide things into those we can control, and those we cannot. Within our power are our character and judgement, but beyond our exclusive control are the goals of health, wealth and renown.

The way to happiness, says Epictetus, is to limit our desires to the areas we *can* control, and to teach ourselves to acquiesce in those we cannot. Wealth and pleasure cannot be good in themselves, for they do not benefit all who experience them; they can be only of instrumental assistance. But living the life of reason, and living virtuously according to nature, is always good.

People can teach themselves imperturbability and freedom from passion; they can render themselves invulnerable to what fate and circumstance bring their way, and this comes only through self-discipline and knowledge. 'We are disturbed not by events,' Epictetus observes, 'but by the views which we take of them.' The word 'ataraxia' describes this goal of indifferent serenity.

Epictetus believed in the brotherhood of humankind, and that living in accord with virtue includes acceptance of social responsibility and duties towards others. He himself taught ordinary people, not just the rich and famous, although the Emperor Hadrian featured among his visitors.

The Stoicism of Epictetus is not about passive acceptance of unhappiness, but a conviction that people can mould their character to become indifferent to circumstances which bring unhappiness to less disciplined people. He practised restraint himself, with a modest, simple lifestyle. He was unmarried, but in old age he adopted and raised a friend's child that would otherwise have died.

22. Ptolemy
c AD 85–c 165

Claudius Ptolemaeus is principally known for the Ptolemaic System, a model of the universe which has a fixed earth at the centre, with sun, moon, planets and stars revolving around it in concentric spheres.

Greek by origin, but living in the Roman province of Egypt, Ptolemy's fame rests on three major treatises, on Astronomy, Geography and Astrology, though he also wrote on music and optics and was an accomplished mathematician.

Ptolemy's most celebrated work was *The Mathematical Collection*, known to us by its Arabic name *The Almagest* (greatest compilation), finished about AD 150. In it Ptolemy sets out the mathematics of his model, complete with tables that enable the positions of the planets to be calculated accurately enough for the unaided observer. The work, preserved by Arab scholars, was used as a practical text for 1,400 years. It is a highly sophisticated mathematical model to fit observational data derived from Hipparchus and his successors. It uses eccentric circles and epicycles and incorporates new equations and theorems to provide reasonably accurate predictions. The initial Copernican heliocentric alternative actually generated less accurate predictions until Kepler's Laws were added, and was preferred for its simplicity, not its accuracy.

The Almagest also featured a catalogue of over 1,000 stars and descriptions of 48 constellations. Ptolemy calculated the sphere of the sun's motion to be 1,210 times the earth's radius distant, whereas that of the stars was 20,000 times the earth's radius away. The model of a static earth nesting within concentric spheres accorded with the Church's view of it as the centre of God's creation.

Ptolemy also produced a map of the known world, with the coordinates of places marked on a grid. He knew the earth was a sphere, and was aware that he knew less than half of it. Errors in his calculations, based on insufficient data, distorted his map, and he had Asia extending much further east than it did – which some think influenced Columbus in his choice of a westward journey.

His work on astrology, *Tetrabiblios* (four books), like his other works, gathered the work of earlier writers into a more systematic presentation. Ptolemy thought of it as an empirical science, a collection of data used to cast horoscopes, though he knew it was imprecise.

Part of Ptolemy's significance is that for centuries his work was taken as a true description of the heavens and the earth. It was only with the Renaissance that scholars were emboldened to challenge and supplant his ideas.

23. Marcus Aurelius
AD 121–180

The historian Edward Gibbon equated the period in which people had been most happy and prosperous with the rule of the five Stoic Roman emperors. These five – Nerva, Trajan, Hadrian, Antoninus Pius and Marcus Aurelius – combined personal abstinence and endurance with a dedication to public duty. Marcus Aurelius, the last of these, wrote down his thoughts in a journal as he went about the business of the empire, much of it from military camps. Published long after his death as his *Meditations*, it is regarded as a classic exposition of the Stoic philosophy in practice.

Marcus Aurelius came early to Stoicism. At 17, when adopted and designated as his successor by Antoninus Pius, he had already been educated by the great scholars of his day. A borrowed copy of the discourses of Epictetus formed the foundation for many of his own beliefs. The philosophy, named after the *Stoa Poikile* (painted porch) in which Zeno originally taught it, held the pantheistic view that the universe was God, and that humans were part of it.

The aim of life should be to live in harmony with the universe, detaching oneself from transitory worldly pleasures, and seeking instead the inner calm which comes to a mind devoted to reason. The *Meditations* of Marcus Aurelius are the jottings he wrote down in his quest for self-improvement. His aim was, through a series of mental exercises, to make himself a better person. The important thing was not what a person was, but how he behaved, and each day he tried to train himself to behave better. 'Even in a palace,' he wrote, 'life may be lived well.'

He lists the qualities he has learned from others, including his family. The list includes such virtues as control of temper, abstinence, simplicity, steadiness of purpose and self-government. With the Pax Romana steadily dissolving as Rome's frontiers crumbled, a philosophy that taught duty, self-discipline and endurance seemed appropriate to the times.

It was also a philosophy suited to a vast and varied empire. It taught that each person was part of the divine universe, and therefore linked to all other people. Aurelius wrote of 'one soul distributed among several natures'.

Aurelius sought inner freedom by submitting to providence, and by cultivating indifference to what he could not influence. Death held no fear for him since he believed in no personal immortality, but thought 'Every part of me will be reduced by change into some part of the universe.'

24. Sextus Empiricus
   AD 160–210

Sextus Empiricus, despite his name, was more of a sceptic than an empiricist. A Greek philosopher of the Roman Empire, Sextus flourished in Alexandria and Athens in the second century AD. He trained as a doctor, but is remembered for his elegant collection of arguments for the sceptic position, a significant portion of which survive.

His three-book collection, *Outlines of Pyrrhonism*, sets out arguments supporting the position taken by Pyrrho of Elis some 500 years earlier. Sextus follows Pyrrho in urging that there can be no certain knowledge of truth or falsity, and that the only defensible position is to suspend judgment.

Sextus also wrote a series of works arguing against the positions taken in various disciplines. The collection was called *Against the Mathematicians*, with the first six books commonly known as *Against the Professors*. He targets grammar, rhetoric, geometry, mathematics, astrology and music, with five more of its books arguing against logicians, physicists and ethicists. He clearly did not avoid dispute.

Sextus identifies three different types of philosophy. There are Dogmatists, who think they knew the truth. There are Academic Sceptics, who think that truth can never be known. Then there are Sceptics, who retain an open mind, not thinking truth is yet discovered, but prepared to accept that it might be.

For each proposed truth, said Sextus, there is an equally compelling opposite and incompatible one, and an aloof scepticism is the only valid response to their competing claims. Furthermore, each claim to truth must appeal to some standard of truth, which in turn must appeal to a higher one, leading to an infinite regress.

The evidence of our senses is subjective, in that men and animals perceive things differently, and perceptions differ between different men. The perceptions vary at different times and places, too, and change with colours and temperatures. They cannot be related to any external reality. It is not that appearances and perceptions do not exist, just that we have to suspend judgment about what their true nature might be. Honey, for example, is called sweet, but the sweetness is not in the honey, but in our perception of it.

To Sextus, scepticism brought peace of mind ('ataraxia') by the realization that truth could not be known, and by suspending judgment about it. Having no knowledge of what is objectively good, the sceptic feels no disquiet at falling short of it. He suspends judgement not only about ethics, but even about the reality of matter, time and space.

25. Plotinus
c AD 205–270

Plotinus founded the philosophy called Neoplatonism, regarded as sufficiently attractive to vie with Christianity in the Roman world. Plotinus, born in Egypt, became a teacher of philosophy in Rome, achieving a celebrity status that included the admiration of emperors. We know his thought through the *Enneads*, six sets of nine books edited from his notes and published after his death by his disciple Porphyry.

Plotinus lived an ascetic life of which Porphyry said, 'he seemed ashamed to be in his body'. Despite his emphasis on the contemplative life and the mysticism he added to Platonism, Plotinus was apparently a practical man, appointed guardian to the children of friends who died.

The divine cosmology of Plotinus has the universe as a succession of realities, each of which derives from the one above it, and gives existence to the one below. At the apex is the 'One', that which is perfect and complete, with no attributes and no parts to mar its unity. It is not even self-conscious, for that would require the duality of self and consciousness. It is simply the supreme goodness, corresponding with Plato's idea of 'the Good'.

Below it is the world of 'Intelligence' (or 'Mind'), created by an emanation, or overflow, from the One, as light comes from the sun. It is the world of ideas conceived of in the mind of the One, and is equivalent to the domain of Plato's 'Absolute Forms' of things.

Next comes the world of 'Soul', created by the emanation from the higher world of Intelligence. It contemplates things successively, thus creating time and space, but is itself eternal. It in turn generates the world of 'Nature', with individual souls. This is more inferior because it is further from the One.

Finally, at the lowest level, is the material world. Each person has elements of matter, nature, soul and intelligence, and can, says Plotinus, reach up to the various levels by contemplation and self-discipline. It is even possible by supreme intellectual effort to reach briefly to the level of the One, experiencing the ecstasy of supreme unity and self-sufficiency. Plotinus said he had experienced this ecstasy four times during his life.

Parallels with Christianity are evident. Some of his followers gave their wealth to the poor and led lives of contemplation, trying to purify their minds to ascend the hierarchy of worlds. And the insistence of Plotinus that happiness comes from inner contemplation, not the material world, influenced St Augustine and early Christian doctrine.

26. Saint Augustine of Hippo
AD 354–430

St Augustine of Hippo profoundly influenced the course of Christianity during the decay of the Western Roman Empire. His thinking is a bridge between the classical scholarship of Greece and Rome and the ideas of mediaeval Christianity. As a late convert to Catholicism, he was ordained a bishop in Roman Africa, and set out in over 100 publications what were to become definitive Church positions on original sin and the Church's relationship to the world around it.

He took Plato's separation of the transient, imperfect world of material things from the eternal, perfect world accessible by intellect, and applied it to Christian theology. His book *The City of God* (from AD 413) describes how that city coexists with the City of Men. The world of the senses is contrasted with the much larger reality of God's eternal world. The City of God on earth is the Church, more specifically the company of the elect who are granted eternal life. All others, including non-baptized infants, suffer eternal fiery torment. The City of Men will perish, but the City of God will endure.

The idea that the Church coexisted with, but was separate from, the political state set the future for Church–state relationships in mediaeval Europe, with the Church achieving primacy in religious matters. While the political world was dissolving into chaos as barbarians invaded and sacked the Western Roman Empire, Augustine's ideas provided the means for people to endure and accept earthly suffering, and concentrate upon the spiritual matters which promised eternity.

Augustine took a pessimistic view of original sin. He thought all men deserved to burn in hell because of it, but a few were chosen to be saved by God's grace. There was nothing people could do join the elect; it was God's choice and was pre-determined. This was reconciled with free will because God, being present throughout time, knew what people would freely choose. Some of these ideas later featured in Calvinism during the Reformation.

In his *Confessions* (AD 397), still widely read, Augustine describes the development of his ideas through his life. He particularly denounces lust, acknowledging his own earlier failings on that score. What is particularly bad about it is that, in the grip of lustful passions, men lose control. He himself abandoned both his long-time partner and his betrothed on his conversion, and led a celibate, churchly life. A prayer of his youth is still quoted today, however: 'Grant me chastity and continence, but not yet.'

27. St Anselm
1033–1109

St Anselm is regarded as the father of scholasticism, the philo-sophy which dominated mediaeval thinking until the Renais-sance. Anselm sought to reconcile reason with faith. Reason was not a substitute for faith, he maintained, but could lead people to understand what was first accepted through faith.

Born in Burgundy, Anselm became Archbishop of Canterbury in the period after the Norman conquest. He was virtually forced into the post by a king who had experienced conflict from his predecessor. Anselm himself proved no easier a partner, his tenure spent in regal disputes over papal authority. But it is Anselm's theological and philosophical writing which established his reputation.

He offered carefully thought-out proofs for the existence of God. In his *Monologion*, *Proslogion* and *De Veritate* he sets out chains of reasoning which conclude in the existence of an almighty being, although he cautions that 'Unless I first believe, I shall not understand.'

His first proof is that if we are to call things good, great or just, there must be some standard against which we can measure such things. Our understanding of such terms implies the exis-tence of one supremely good, great and just thing, through which other things have these qualities.

Anselm further says that things would not exist without something through which they came to exist, since nothing can exist through nothing. This something exists through itself, and is therefore 'greatest and supreme among all existing things'.

The proof which attracted most attention is that which Kant dubbed the 'ontological' proof. It asks if we can conceive of 'that than which nothing greater can be conceived of'. This must have reality, otherwise it would be possible to conceive of a greater thing – that which had real existence as well.

Anselm went on from deducing the existence of a supreme being to eliciting the attributes with which Christianity equips it, including infinite power and wisdom, and he explained the necessity of free will, redemption, the Trinity and the incarnation.

Anselm's contemporary, the monk Gaunilo, was the first to cast doubt on this type of reasoning, asking how ideas in the mind could lead to the world of real existence. He also mocked Anselm's ontological proof, pointing out that one might just as easily imagine an island 'than that no greater island could be conceived of', and then conceive of one greater by virtue of its real existence.

Despite such controversy, Anselm made an influential and lasting contribution to Christian theology by pointing how reason could follow intelligently where faith had led.

28. Roger Bacon
c 1214–1294

Bacon was an early exponent of scientific method. At a time when knowledge was gained by reading classical texts and using deductive reasoning, Bacon urged the primacy of experiment. 'Reasoning draws a conclusion,' he said, 'but does not make the conclusion certain, unless the mind discovers it by the path of experience.'

As a Franciscan friar he had to be cautious lest such sentiments incur the wrath of his order's authorities. His opening came when his friend Cardinal de Foulques became Pope Clement IV and commissioned him to write about philosophy. His response was his *Opus Majus*, followed by *Opus Minus* and *Opus Tertium*. He wrote about Aristotle, now accessible to him in the original Greek, and the new science.

Bacon had lectured at the University of Paris, then an intellectual hub, and was acquainted with and influenced by some of the leading minds of his day. He also read the work of Arab scholars, especially mathematicians and scientists. His own writing covered a large range of subjects, including alchemy, astronomy and optics as well as mathematics. He wrote about spectacles and telescopes before these became practical instruments. He worked on mirrors, too, and identifed the spectrum produced by shining white light through a glass of water.

He described the manufacture of gunpowder, and understood that it would explode with great force if confined. He speculated on flying machines, including ones that would move by flapping mechanical wings. He wrote how ships and carriages might be propelled by mechanical power. He did calculations on the position of celestial objects, and advocated reform of the calendar. Although he had a laboratory, he tended to describe experiments rather than to perform them, but his emphasis was on the primacy of empirical research.

He identified four stumbling blocks which kept people from the truth. These were 'weak and unworthy authority, long-standing custom, the feeling of the ignorant crowd, and the hiding of our own ignorance while making a display of our apparent knowledge'. Experimental science, on the other hand, had three great virtues in his eyes. It verifies conclusions by direct experiment; it discovers new truths; and it investigates secrets of nature and opens up knowledge of the past and the future.

Some of Bacon's thinking sat ill with Church and Franciscan authorities, and Bacon was charged with 'novelties' and impri-soned for a time, though he survived unscathed and lived to be 80. His ideas have lived even longer.

29. Thomas Aquinas
c 1225–1274

Thomas Aquinas lived at a critical junction for Christian thought. The first universities were being founded, and the works of Aristotle were becoming widely available in the West from Arabic sources. The Aristotelian approach gave knowledge through reason, whereas Christianity derived it from faith and revelation. The disjunction threatened to undermine theology, but Aquinas developed a synthesis of the two which became the basis of Christian philosophy. He is said to have 'baptized' Aristotle.

Aquinas studied as a boy at Monte Cassino, but when he became a Dominican at 16, his family locked him in a tower for a year until he escaped. He became known as the 'dumb ox' because of his portly build, and it was said that 'his bellowing will fill the world'. His works were censured, but later rehabilitated, and he was canonized five years after his death.

Faith and reason were separate, said Aquinas, but complemented and did not contradict each other. Reason could show God's existence and attributes, but doctrines such as the Trinity and the incarnation were revealed through revelation. Taking Aristotle's account of physical objects, sense perception and intellectual knowledge, Aquinas applied them to Christian purposes, developing five proofs for the existence of God.

1. God is the first mover, the cause of motion in others.
2. He is the first cause that causes all other things.
3. He is the one non-contingent, necessary, being which underlies the existence of contingent things.
4. He is the greatest being from which lesser great things derive their greatness.
5. He is the intelligent designer who directs non-intelligent things to act towards an end.

By harnessing reason and faith together, Aquinas was able to transform Aristotle's distant and impersonal prime mover into the Christian idea of a God who enters people's lives and cares for them individually. 'For the knowledge of any truth whatsoever, man needs divine help,' he taught, but God has given men reason, and they use it to gain knowledge by way of their senses, as Aristotle had taught.

Aquinas was a systematic thinker. He identified the four cardinal virtues: prudence, temperance, justices and fortitude; and he listed the three theological virtues of faith, hope, and charity. He describes the divine nature of God in five attributes: He is simple, not made up of parts. He is perfect, infinite, immutable, and He is one, an undivided unity.

The philosophy and theology of Aquinas (called 'Thomism') have dominated Church thinking since, earning him the soubriquet 'Dr Angelicus'.

30. William of Occam (Ockham)
c 1287–1347

Famous for the maxim called 'Occam's Razor', William of Occam was a remarkable and original fourteenth-century thinker. A Franciscan friar, he studied at Oxford after his ordination without completing his degree. He must already have demonstrated original thought, for Oxford's chancellor levied charges of heresy against him, and he was summoned to Avignon to answer to Pope John XXII. The head of the Franciscan order was also summoned to answer heresy charges for proclaiming that followers of Jesus should renounce property and live by begging, and William did not help his own case by siding with his leader and charging the Pope himself with heresy. The Franciscans fled at night to the protection of Emperor Louis IV of Bavaria.

In his greatest work, *Summa Logicae* (c 1323), William put his own stamp onto traditional Aristotelian and scholastic philosophy. He denied Aristotle's self-evident principles, and took the view that humans perceive objects directly through 'intuitive cognition', without the intervention of innate ideas. He postulated that only individual things exist, and denied that there were any 'real' forms or essences or universals underlying appearances. On the contrary, he said, these were merely abstractions created by the human mind, and were no more than a way of thinking about several things at once. This position, called nominalism, ran counter to the thinking of his day.

'Occam's Razor' is the name given to a maxim which rejects unnecessarily complicated explanations. Occam did not invent it, but his exposition and use of it forever links it with his name. It reflects the 'principle of parsimony' in explanation, and says that if one can explain without assuming hypothetical entities, one has no grounds to assume them. Occam expressed it thus: 'For nothing ought to be posited without a reason given, unless it is self-evident [literally, known through itself] or known by experience or proved by the authority of Sacred Scripture.'

One should take the simplest explanation that actually explains, says Occam; further assumptions are unnecessary and unjustified. The principle is often summed up as 'entities must not be multiplied beyond necessity', although Occam never used those words. Occam's Razor is a rule of thumb, and does not prove things wrong. He himself used it to suspend judgment, rather than to disprove or deny things. It stops people from supposing things they have no reason to suppose.

Just as controversially, Occam rejected any link between faith and reason, dismissing proposed proofs of God's existence, and claiming that belief in God must rest on faith alone, unsupported by reason and argument.

31. Francesco Petrarch
1304–1374

Francesco Petrarch was a pivotal figure at the cusp between mediaeval and modern thinking. He has been called father of the Renaissance, father of humanism, and even the father of mountaineering. An Italian writer, poet and philosopher, he rescued from neglect the writers of the pre-Christian classical era, and integrated their ideas into the contemporary world view.

Petrarch was a celebrated figure of his day. He had studied for the legal profession, but despised it, preferring instead to write Latin poetry, though two of his most famous works, *Canzoniere* and *Triumphs*, were in Italian, bringing it a new elegance. His epic *Africa*, about the Roman general Scipio Africanus, brought Petrarch renown, and in 1341 he was crowned poet laureate at a ceremony in Rome, the first to hold the title for a thousand years. Significantly, he placed his laurel crown on the tomb of St Peter, symbolizing the union of the classical and Christian worlds.

In 1336 he climbed Mount Ventoux. Unlike his predecessors, he did it for pleasure, and was thrilled by the scenic grandeur. He wrote about his experiences in vivid terms, becoming the first modern mountaineer. The mediaeval attitude commonly regarded life as but a wretched preparation for the glorious afterlife, but Petrarch valued earthly life and its experiences, believing that intellect and creativity were God-given and should be exulted in. These ideas set the stage for the Renaissance and its values.

In 1345 he discovered some hitherto unknown letters of Cicero at Verona, and began a search for the neglected writings of the ancients, travelling widely. He castigated the neglect of scholarship, coining the term 'Dark Ages' to describe the mediaeval period. He wrote, 'Each famous author of antiquity whom I recover places a new offence and another cause of dishonour to the charge of earlier generations.' The discoveries inspired Petrarch to write his own letters to some of these thinkers of old.

His experience of love was a profound inspiration for his poetry. He was intoxicated by a girl, Laura, he saw in a church in 1327. She was already married, so Petrarch chanelled his passion into a series of intensely lyrical love poems known as the *Canzoniere*, which defined the Italian sonnet and influenced generations of writers who followed. She died of the plague in 1348, and Petrarch expressed his grief and despair in his poetry.

His concern with human experiences instead of only religious themes marked the beginning of the Renaissance and the emergence of modern thought.

32. Desiderius Erasmus
c 1466–1536

Desiderius Erasmus was a Dutch scholar whose life and work bridged the gap between the mediaeval and modern worlds. Although as a young man he was reluctantly inducted into a monastery and ordained as a priest, he chose instead a life of scholarship, publishing extensively and corresponding with the leading thinkers of his day.

Although the Church preached submission to its authority, Erasmus instead subjected its practices to critical analysis, using reason instead of unthinking acquiescence to examine their strength and validity. He criticized the contemporary Church for its reliance on superstition and empty tradition, and advocated instead a rational piety. In opposition to some Church leaders who feared that knowledge would lead people to stray from their faith, Erasmus said that it would instead give their religious beliefs a secure foundation. He is regarded as a leading humanist thinker who helped liberate people from the darkness of superstition.

The printing press, now spreading across Europe, gave Erasmus the opportunity to support himself from scholarship, and he published many best-selling works, including the first printed New Testament in Greek. His rigorous research produced more accurate versions of classical texts, which he used to urge a return to the scriptures, and the abandonment of the rituals which characterized worship at the time. By insisting that individuals could judge on such matters, rather than going through the authority of the Church and its priesthood, he was running counter to the traditional teachings of the Catholic Church.

He wrote *In Praise of Folly* as a satire on the excesses in which bishops and monks indulged, engaging in some of the criticism of their opulence which led Martin Luther and others to launch the Reformation. Although Erasmus denounced reliance on holy relics, ceremonies, pilgrimages, and the other ways in which the Church fed popular superstition, he himself never supported the Protestant Reformation, preferring instead to spread his ideas within the Catholic Church. He tried to keep aloof from the increasingly bitter religious disputes, but Erasmus's views were regarded with suspicion by Catholics and Protestants alike.

In his *Handbook of a Christian Knight*, Erasmus urged study and contemplation as a means to true Christian virtue. But his denunciation of the Church's practices and his use of scholarship to challenge its authority helped to weaken the grip of its leadership over the minds of men and women. It was said that Erasmus laid the egg which Luther hatched, and which gave birth to the Reformation.

33. Niccolo Machiavelli
1469–1527

Few people see their names pass into language, and very few seek the fate that befell Niccolo Machiavelli. The word 'Machiavellian' is used for those who are deceitful, machinating and cunning.

Machiavelli was closely involved in the politics and conflicts of Italy's independent city states. His native Florence became a republic, and Machiavelli served as secretary to its Chancery, undertaking diplomatic missions and observing how effectively various rulers practised government. His own political career was unsuccessful, in that the Medici family retook Florence and imprisoned and tortured Machiavelli. His response was his writing. His *Discourses on Livy* (1531) conveyed his own preference for self-governing states, though it is *The Prince* (1513) which made his name and posthumous reputation.

In the form of a letter to Lorenzo de Medici, this work sets out the maxims by which a prince should seek to rule successfully. What gives Machiavelli his status as a founder of political philosophy is that he breaks completely with the earlier tradition of seeking wise and just governments. Machiavelli is more brutally realistic. To him governance is about seizing and holding power, and doing whatever it takes to do so successfully.

It is easy, he says, to hold onto an hereditary state. All the ruler need do is keep its customs and act prudently. It is harder to seize power and establish a secure new rule. It helps if you start by murdering the previous ruling family. The prince sometimes needs to act cruelly in order to inspire fear, and should do so quickly and decisively. Benefits, on the other hand, should be eked out slowly so their goodwill lasts longer.

Deception plays a key role because people see only the appearances, and the vulgar are always taken in by them. Rulers have to be brutal, even evil, he advises, because force is successful, whereas virtue is not, but the ruler should feign virtue to avoid incurring hatred.

Machiavelli, who himself wrote on *The Art of War* (1520), says a ruler should have no other study. He should maintain a strong army and not rely on mercenaries or auxiliaries who can turn against him.

Machiavelli illustrates his points with copious examples drawn from the turbulent politics of his day, but his model was the brutal and amoral Cesare Borgia. This was strong stuff, and Machiavelli was not himself restored to princely favour. His stark insights into power have made his name endure, however, though as a byword for devious duplicity.

34. Galileo Galilei
1564–1642

In 1610 a slim volume, *The Starry Messenger*, appeared, and changed the world as much as any publication. The author was Galileo Galilei of Pisa in Italy. He had heard of the telescope, invented in the Netherlands in 1608, and constructed his own with superior magnification, learning to grind and polish lenses to make it better still. He demonstrated it to the merchants of Pisa to spot ships returning from sea, with commercial implications. Then he turned it to the heavens.

In *The Starry Messenger* he described how he had observed four moons circling Jupiter. The prevailing geocentric view deriving from Aristotle and Ptolemy and taught by the Church had the earth at the centre of the universe. Jupiter's four moons implied a non-geocentric view, while Galileo's observation of the phases of Venus lent support to the Copernican model, with the sun at the centre. Galileo reported the mountains and craters his telescope had revealed on the moon, making it a rough world rather than the 'perfect sphere' described by Aristotle. And sunspots revealed not only imperfections on the sun, but also its rotation.

Galileo had earlier considered a career in the Church, but chose medicine instead, before switching to mathematics and becoming a professor at 25. He was adept at mechanics, too, contradicting Aristotle's claim that heavier weights fell faster by allegedly dropping balls from Pisa's leaning tower. He reportedly timed the swing of a cathedral chandelier with his pulse to decide that a pendulum swing took the same time regardless of its arc of swing.

Galileo was using observation and reasoning based on it to learn about nature, rather than accepting authority, either of the ancient writers or of the Church. In doing so he angered the Church hierarchy and from 1616 was forbidden to teach

Copernican ideas. He still managed to publish *The Assayer* in 1623, a defence of scientific method and of understanding nature through the language of mathematics. Einstein called him 'the father of modern science'.

In 1633, Galileo was tried and convicted of heresy. Then aged 69 and frail, he was shown the instruments of torture and made to recant his belief that the earth moves around the sun. He spent his remaining years under house arrest, forbidden to teach or publish, and went blind at age 75. Two hundred years after Galileo's trial the Church finally removed Copernican ideas from its index of banned works, and in 1992, Pope John Paul II finally apologized to Galileo on its behalf.

35. Thomas Hobbes
1588–1679

Thomas Hobbes' life changed at age 40 as he waited in a gentleman's library and saw a copy of Euclid's *Geometry* open at Pythagoras' Theorem. 'By God, 'tis impossible!' he allegedly exclaimed, but found himself referred to earlier proofs and eventually to first principles. Finally satisfied, he wondered if he might bring the same approach to bear in politics. He admired Galileo and Kepler's scientific method, and wanted to apply it to social studies. The result was *Leviathan* (1651), a systematic account of the origins of civil government, and a major work of political philosophy.

Hobbes starts his first principles by imagining men and women in a state of nature, before civil society. It is a wretched state, he observes, a state of war with everyone fighting each other for self-defence and dominance. There is no industry, no farming, no trade and no arts, and the life of man, he famously said, 'is solitary, poor, nasty, brutish and short'.

People act in their own interest, he said, calling whatever they like 'good', and what they avoid 'bad'. They act as their own judge and jury in disputes, making it a war of all against all. To escape this damaging chaos, people agree to accept a sovereign. They agree to relinquish authority and judgement over their own lives, accepting instead a powerful ruler over all of them.

Unlike Locke, who later described a social contract between people and their government, Hobbes has it only between the people; the sovereign is not part of it and cedes no authority. Hobbes therefore sees the sovereign as having absolute power. The separation of powers later described by Locke and Montesquieu, and integral to the US Constitution, does not feature in Hobbes' account. On the contrary, the sovereign must exercise undivided powers to ensure effective government. The only limit on the sovereign's absolute power is that people retain the right to protect themselves when their lives are threatened.

Hobbes lived through the bloody English Civil War, and fled to Paris with many of the Royalists. He was convinced that only an all-powerful government could contain the discord and chaos which he had witnessed. *Leviathan* was disliked by the Royalists, however, for its anti-Catholic, secular tone. It was equally disliked by the Parliamentarians for its justification of absolute monarchy. Hobbes was partly restored to favour with the restoration to the throne of Charles II, to whom he had taught mathematics whilst in Paris.

36. René Descartes
1596–1650

Descartes is the first 'modern' philosopher because he broke with the mediaeval scholastic philosophy based on Aristotle, and tried to establish certain truths derived from reasoning.

French born, Descartes chose to live and work in the Dutch Republic. *Le Monde* was to have been his first book in 1634, but was hastily stopped when news came of Galileo's trial for heresy and house imprisonment as Descartes had also embraced the Copernican system. It was only published posthumously, and it was instead called *Discourse on Method* (1637) which established his reputation.

Descartes wanted to avoid anything open to doubt. The evidence of his own senses was uncertain because he might be dreaming. Using methodic (or 'hyperbolic') doubt to reject everything uncertain, Descartes begins with one clear and certain truth. He is thinking, so his thinking self exists. This is the famous 'cogito ergo sum' (that is, 'I think, therefore I am') on which Descartes builds his system. He has intuitively sure knowledge of his own existence or he would not be thinking.

He then says that all ideas as clear and distinct as this one must be true, for if any in that class were to be uncertain, the cogito itself might be uncertain. Descartes adds to his clear and distinct idea of God the ontological argument of St Anselm (that our idea of a perfect being must include its real existence). Furthermore, since God leads him to suppose that things in the world outside him are material, they must be so because a perfect God would not deceive him. Descartes' reason, not perception, tells him he can trust sensory evidence.

Knowing that a piece of wax can change all its sensory properties while still remaining the same piece of wax, Descartes deduces that this knowledge must come from his mind, not his senses. He deduces that mind is mental substance, while body is material substance. This is Cartesian dualism, the separation between a non-material mind and a mechanistic body. The mind, which Descartes thought located in the pineal gland, directs the body, but there can be feedback from the body.

Gassendi, in criticism, asked what point of contact ('surfaces') enable a non-material mind to move a material body. And Arnaud claimed it was circular reasoning to say that God exists because we have a clear and distinct idea of Him, which in turn is guaranteed by God.

Outside of epistemology, Descartes revolutionized mathematics by introducing algebra into geometry, thus developing coordinate ('Cartesian') geometry.

37. Blaise Pascal
1623–1662

The life of Blaise Pascal testifies that the quality of a human life is not measured in years or in happiness. He died shortly after his 39th birthday, after a lifetime of sickness and suffering. Yet in that short life he proved himself one of Western civilization's greatest intellects, making original contributions in mathematics, physics and religious thought.

A childhood prodigy taught by his father, Pascal replicated theorems by Pythagoras, and at 13 discovered an error in the new geometry of Descartes. At 16 he wrote an influential essay setting out Pascal's Theorem on the plane figures derived from conic sections.

Still in his late teens, Pascal produced a mechanical calculator to aid his father with tax accounting; and his mathematical innovations included Pascal's Triangle, a binomial coefficient table shaped as such. From letters between Pascal and Fermat, probability theory was developed, originally to aid gambling calculations.

In hydrostatics he developed Pascal's Law, that fluids transmit equally in all directions, and invented the hydraulic press. He challenged Descartes by showing that a vacuum could exist, at the top of an inverted column of mercury, and showed by experiment that the size of that vacuum varied with altitude.

Philosophically, Pascal held that truths could be derived from earlier truths, but the first principles themselves were intuitive and could not be proved. This led him to religion as the basis for their acceptance. He embraced Jansenism and argued for it in his *Lettres Provinciales* (1656–7). These 18 letters purported to be from a Parisian to his country friend and had a polished style that won literary acclaim. His witty attacks on Jesuits proved too much for the French king, who had them burnt.

Two religious experiences – a near death experience in a

bridge accident, and a miracle cure for his niece's eye ailment –
reinforced Pascal's religious commitment, to which he devoted
his later years. His final work, published posthumously as the
Pensées, was hailed as a masterpiece of French literature and an
inspiration to believers. Compiled from his notes, it defends
Christianity, glorying in God's awesome power. Pascal distinguishes between the mathematical and the intuitive mind, which
rarely mix. 'The heart has its reasons, of which reason knows
nothing,' he wrote, describing the intuitive nature of a faith-
centred belief. He applied probability theory to formulate Pascal's famous wager: 'If God does not exist, one will lose nothing
by believing in him, while if he does exist, one will lose everything by not believing.'

38. John Locke
1632–1704

John Locke is a major figure in two important areas of philosophy. He was a leading exponent of the empirical theory of knowledge, and a seminal contributor to the contract theory of civil government.

He was raised during the violent discord of the English Civil War. A trained doctor, he became personal physician to the powerful Earl of Shaftesbury, and acted as his trade secretary for a spell. Forced to flee the Stuart monarchy, he used his time abroad to write the works he published when the Glorious Revolution of 1688 replaced James II's autocratic rule with the constitutional government of William and Mary.

His *Two Treatises on Civil Government* (1690) provide justification for the Glorious Revolution. He draws on the twin themes of natural rights and social contract. Locke is determined to refute any 'divine right of kings', and to establish that government is not 'merely the product of force and violence'.

In a state of nature, which Locke thought rooted in history, people have the right to self-preservation by protecting their life, health and property. People acquire property rights by 'mixing their labour' with God's gifts, such as by picking berries. It is illegitimate to acquire more than they can use without it spoiling, but agriculture and money have enabled the surplus property of some to be used by others.

These rights pre-date government, but without civil society, people act as their own judge in disputes. To resolve conflicts and protect their rights, people contract to form governments whose duty is to preserve their rights to life, health and property. Government rules with the explicit consent of the governed, and becomes illegitimate if it violates these rights, putting itself in a state of war with its citizens and justifying its overthrow. Locke's principles became very influential in both the American and French revolutions.

In Locke's *Essay Concerning Human Understanding* (1690), he seeks to discover how our ideas enter our minds. Whence comes our knowledge? Ultimately, he says, from sensory experiences. We have no innate ideas, or we would be aware of them immediately. Instead our mind is a tabula rasa into which some ideas come from sensation, some from reflection. Simple ideas come from sensory experience, and can be combined in the mind into complex ones, but there is nothing in the intellect that did not enter through the senses. The primacy Locke gave to empirical data fitted well with burgeoning scientific discoveries and a new understanding of the scientific method.

39. Benedict de Spinoza
1632–1677

Benedict de Spinoza incurred obloquy in his day and for years afterwards for his heretical religious views, but is now regarded as a pillar of seventeenth-century rationalism. His departure from the conventional views of his Jewish upbringing led to a *cherem*, or excommunication, against him while still in his early twenties. He lived in the Netherlands working as a lens grinder, but devoted his life to the study of ideas.

His first publication, on Descartes, was the only one in his lifetime done under his own name. His views were known and discussed during his life, but he wisely published his *Theologico-political Treatise* (1670) anonymously, and his greatest work, *Ethics* (1676), was published posthumously. The views that aroused such outrage were his reasonings on God and the universe.

Rejecting the dualism of mind and body propounded by Descartes, Spinoza concluded that there was only one reality in nature, one substance behaving according to one set of rules. This single substance was nature (the universe), which equated with God, and was both infinite and perfect. Everything in it, including people, were but aspects ('modes') of it. Furthermore, it proceeded according to its own necessity, without space for chance or for human free will.

Spinoza rejected the notion of an anthropomorphic God with a personality. His pantheistic God, the natural world, took no interest in the fate or actions of humans, and was thoroughly deterministic. Men suppose they have free will, but only because they do not understand the causes which determine their actions.

Spinoza's moral views were equally radical. There is no objective good or evil, he said, because these are terms relating to our perceptions, not to reality. We see things as disasters or injustices only because of our inability to perceive things properly. The universe is perfect, but we are unable to see this.

Happiness comes not through worldly goods or passions but through a life of reason, and the highest virtue comes through knowledge of God (the universe). Spinoza thus advocated a life not dissimilar from Stoicism, in which mere worldly pleasures were forsaken for intellectual understanding of ourselves and nature, leading to control over our desires. 'True virtue is life under the direction of reason.'

Spinoza himself lived a commendably simple and contemplative life, refusing offers of honour or advancement, preferring instead to study and practise philosophy. He died young from a lung ailment possibly caused by glass powder inhaled in his work.

40. Isaac Newton
1643–1727

Newton has, more than anyone, changed the way people think about their world. Born, symbolically, on Christmas Day in the year of Galileo's death, Newton showed that the world could be understood because it followed rational laws, and that the same laws which governed the behaviour of nearby objects also regulated the most distant parts of the heavens.

Sent home from Trinity College for the two years when Cambridge closed during the Black Death (Great Plague), Newton contemplated an apple fall in his garden, and wondered why it moved towards the earth's centre rather than in any other direction, and whether the force which impelled it might work at greater distances, even up to the moon and beyond. Urged on by Sir Edmund Halley, the Astronomer Royal, the results of Newton's enquiries were published as *Principia Mathematica* (1687).

It spelled out the three laws of motion: that objects continue at rest or in rectilinear motion unless acted upon by an outside force; that the rate of change of momentum is proportional to that outside force; and that to every action there is an equal and opposite reaction.

Armed with these simple laws it was now possible to calculate both the trajectory of a cannon ball, and the motions of the planets in their orbits. Where there had been two domains of earth and the heavens, there was now one. The idea that humankind could gain knowledge of a rational and ordered universe laid the basis for the intellectual Enlightenment which followed.

Newton showed that natural laws governed the behaviour of light, using a prism to split white lights into its coloured components. Realizing that telescope lenses would always have colour distortion, Newton invented the reflecting telescope that bears his name, grinding the mirror and the eyepieces himself.

He used his mathematical 'fluxions' – differential and integral calculus (invented independently by Leibniz) – to mathematize other physical sciences, and he set out the systematic basis for a scientific method based on observation and experiment.

Regarded as a difficult man, he quarrelled with many leading contemporary scientists, and was as involved in alchemy and biblical exegesis as in science. He was noted for his powers of continuous concentration, even to hours or days at a time. He famously said, 'If I have seen further it is by standing on the shoulders of giants.'

His achievement is summed up in Pope's couplet:

'Nature and Nature's laws lay hid in night:
God said, Let Newton be! and all was light.'

41. Gottfried Wilhelm Leibniz
1646–1716

Gottfried Wilhelm Leibniz is celebrated in several fields. Although he came late to mathematics, his powerful intellect made its mark. He demonstrated a calculating machine to the Royal Society, and co-invented calculus with Sir Isaac Newton (though some alleged he'd earlier seen Newton's work). He also devised the binary system, used in modern computer architecture. Born in Leipzig, he spent most of his life serving the House of Hanover, and at one stage even urged the French king Louis XIV to invade Egypt, hoping to divert his attention from Germany.

In philosophy he tried, like many others, to reconcile an all-powerful deity with the world as it seems to be, and created a logically consistent account of how he thought the universe must operate. Leibniz started with self-evident principles such as the notion that a thing is what it is (the identity principle) and that any proposition which leads to a contradiction must be false (principle of non-contradiction). From such basic steps he deduced, with mathematical-style reasoning, that the ultimate reality in the universe must be mind rather than matter.

According to Leibniz, the universe is composed of 'monads', eternal and incorruptible elements, rather corresponding to the atoms which physical scientists take to be its constituents. Monads, however, differ from atoms in two important respects: they are non-material, like an infinite number of 'souls', and do not interact with each other. Each follows programmed instructions, and behaves as it does at any moment because it is part of its identity that it will do so. To have the complete concept of a monad, said Leibniz, is to know everything that will happen to it. A monad is, he declared, 'pregnant' with the future and 'laden' with the past. If one event appears to cause another, this is an illusion; what is really happening is the monads acting independently and simultaneously. It is like clocks striking simultaneously even though they are not connected. Space and time, like cause and effect, are illusions, said Leibniz. The reality is of independent monads which contain their own past and future, each one like a mirror of the universe. God has willed their pre-established harmony.

Leibniz surmised that God made this universe, though not perfect, the best of all possible ones. This was spoofed by Voltaire in *Candide*, whose characters undergo every calamity including war, rape, earthquakes, piracy, and hanging, only to have Dr Pangloss (representing Leibniz) reciting parrot-like that 'everything is for the best in this best of all possible worlds'.

42. Giambattista Vico
1668–1744

Although Vico was not acclaimed in his day, his works became significant as they became more widely known in the century following his death, and even more so in the twentieth century. He is now regarded as a highly original thinker and a pioneer of the philosophy of history.

He remained outside the mainstream thought of his day because he never accepted Descartes' notion that truth could be gained by observation of clear and distinct ideas. By contrast, Vico argued that truth resulted from action, and that humans could know the truth of things they had created. Mathematics, being a human construct, would admit of certainty, but nature, not created by man, would not. History, because it was created by men and women, could be known.

Vico was somewhat isolated intellectually. He was Professor of Rhetoric at Naples, but never gained the Chair of Jurisprudence he coveted, and was not part of the circle of European intellectuals who corresponded with each other. He published an innovative intellectual autobiography, however, describing the development of his own ideas.

In his *New Science* (1725), Vico advanced the thesis that history was cyclical, and that civilizations and cultures went through successive phases of development. History began, said Vico, with an age of myth and superstition and the power of poetic imagination. It developed into what he called the 'Age of Gods', in which men lived in fear of the supernatural. When tribal leaders banded together for their internal and external security, the 'Age of Heroes' came about, with leaders inspiring people to courage and achievement. This saw the emergence of class divisions between the ruling families and the others (patricians and plebeians). As societies developed constitutional forms of government such as republics, the 'Age of Men' came about, with rights secured for the ordinary people as they brought the aristocrats under the law. As things degenerated into corruption, monarchies succeeded, but ultimately barbarism and anarchy took over once more.

Vico held that all cultures went through these phases, and that their social institutions, such as their literature, laws, politics and philosophy, all progressed through historical stages as civilization developed. The notion that history is leading somewhere, and going through a set pattern instead of being a random series of unrelated events, was a radical idea, one which was later to influence Karl Marx, amongst others. Vico also anticipated modern ideas in his treatment of human knowledge in a social, as opposed to a merely scientific, context.

43. Bernard Mandeville
1670–1733

Bernard Mandeville, Dutch by birth and upbringing, chose to live and work in England. Although a qualified doctor, it was through his controversial writings that he achieved celebrity, even notoriety.

He published *The Grumbling Hive* (1705) which was republished as *The Fable of the Bees* (1714), the title by which it became known. A further edition of 1723 included an essay denouncing charity schools, and was declared 'a public nuisance' by a Grand Jury. This made it widely popular, and Mandeville revelled in the controversy as one moralist after another rose to denounce it.

The work that stirred such unprecedented obloquy was a satirical poem which mocked the pretensions of his day. It tells of a beehive in which selfishness rules, and which prospers through the naked self-interest of its inhabitants. The bees, bemoaning their own lack of morality, are suddenly made virtuous by their god, and calamity ensues. Without greed to drive them, industry and commerce no longer function, and the bees leave to live lives of simple poverty.

The cynical message that Mandeville spelled out is that people are basically wicked, out only for themselves, and driven by passions to gratify various desires. Mandeville takes vice to be the gratification of these selfish drives, and virtue to be that which seeks the betterment of others instead. But since selfishness rules man, there is no real virtue, only the pretence of it.

Fortunately for society, men want others to hold the high opinions they have of themselves, and are given the role model of virtuous lives by skilful politicians, so people feign virtue and consideration of others. Virtue is thus hypocritical, founded on pride and promoted by politicians who 'preach up Publick-spiritedness, that they might reap the Fruits of the Self-denial of others'.

The subtitle of the fable is 'Private Vices, Publick Benefits', illustrating what Mandeville sees as the social utility of greed. To satisfy their own desires, people create employment for others, and big spenders seeking only personal gratification generate opportunities for others by spreading their wealth around, so luxury 'Employ'd a Million of the Poor, And odious Pride a Million more.'

To the moralists of his day it was shocking that vice should be regarded as bringing benefit to society, and that virtue, were it not a sham, would cause its collapse. Despite fierce denunciations, Mandeville's ideas had considerable influence, not least upon Adam Smith, the founding father of economics.

44. Bishop (George) Berkeley
1685–1753

George Berkeley, later bishop of Cloyne in Ireland, was a leading exponent of *idealism*. That is, he said that no material objects exist independently of us. We do not perceive material objects, though we commonly speak as though we do. What we perceive, Berkeley pointed out, are our ideas and sensations. We cannot be sure that there are material objects outside of or beyond that process.

When I perceive a table, what I have is a mental sensation, the idea of a table. I have no direct evidence that a material object extended in three-dimensional space gives rise to that perception. All I have are the sensory impressions of things, their sight, sound, taste, touch and smell. I associate them together into the idea of a table. This is why Berkeley said 'esse est percipi', or 'to be is to be perceived'.

Do objects cease to exist when not being perceived? Does the table disappear when I close the study door, or the tree wink out of existence when I leave the quadrangle? Berkeley said, 'The table I write on, I say, exists, that is, I see and feel it; and if I were out of my study I should say it existed, meaning thereby that if I was in my study I might perceive it, or that some other spirit actually does perceive it.' Berkeley himself leaned toward the view that since God perceives things continuously even when no one else does, they continue to exist. This argument fails to convince atheists, however.

Berkeley's view is consistent and cannot be disproved, even though it is at odds with the common sense view that there is a material world accessible through our senses and which continues in our absence. To those who suppose that our ideas are *like* the physical objects they might represent, Berkeley replied that an idea can only be like another idea. Furthermore, he said, 'Two things cannot be said to be alike or unlike till they have been compared.' We cannot compare an idea with the object it is supposed to represent, for we have no direct awareness of that object.

Berkeley thought that Europe was played out, and that the future lay with the New World. He tried to found a college in Bermuda, but failed to secure funding. The College of California was renamed Berkeley in his honour, but he was also famous for promoting the therapeutic qualities of tar-water.

45. Charles, Baron de Montesquieu
1689–1755

Few political philosophers have had such impact on history as Baron de Montesquieu. Reading the Constitution of the United States is like hearing Montesquieu think aloud.

Montesquieu came from an aristocratic, wealthy background. He married rich, inherited his uncle's fortune and title, and never needed to earn his living. He travelled widely across Europe, noting the contrast in cultures and constitutions, and admiring the English constitutional monarchy in particular.

The *Persian Letters* (1721), which brought him literary acclaim, made humorous observations of European ways by two imaginary Persian visitors. Underlying its ridicule is the fact that people do not see themselves as others see them, and find self-knowledge difficult.

Montesquieu's work on the *Grandeur and Decadence of Rome* (1734) is partly a warning that Rome was a poor model for systems of government. He supplied a better model in his *Spirit of the Laws* (1748), which examined different types of constitution and introduced the separation of powers between different arms of government to put checks and balances on each other.

Instead of preferring one set of laws, Montesquieu said they should take account of the circumstances of societies, including their geography, their industries and their practices. While avoiding utopianism, he did think that most countries could have more liberal and humane laws, and that 'all punishment which is not derived from necessity is tyrannical'.

He examined three types of government: monarchies governed by the principle of honour; republics governed by that of civic virtue; and despotisms governed by fear. Monarchies were governed by established laws, unlike despotisms which were subject to the whim of their ruler. In a democracy, he said, citizens should be educated to identify their own interests with those of their country.

It is in the divisions of administrative power that Montesquieu is most innovative. He separates it into executive, legislative and judicial functions, and urges that they be separate but dependent on each other. The executive should have power to veto acts of the legislature, and the latter should be divided between two chambers, each of which can stop laws made by the other. The judiciary should be independent of both.

Montesquieu's modern appeal is enhanced by his view that commerce is the most legitimate way for countries to enrich themselves, and is a cure for the most destructive prejudices. Less enduring has been his view that climate determines character, making southern nations lethargic and indolent, northern ones stiff and icy, and temperate France best of all.

46. Voltaire (François-Marie Arouet) 1694–1778

Voltaire personified the eighteenth-century European Enlightenment. He lived by his pen, writing poems, essays, plays, novels and letters (20,000 of them). Exiled from France for three years by a disgruntled young nobleman using judicial powers that favoured the aristocracy, Voltaire went to England. He much admired its civil liberties and constitutional government, along with its leading thinkers such as Locke. He returned to publish his *Philosophical Letters on the English* (1734), which sharply criticized France by comparison.

He dedicated his life after that to campaigning for basic freedom, religious tolerance and free trade. Though he did not utter the famous line attributed to him about defending to the death the right of a person he disagreed with to express himself, it does in fact sum up his life's attitude to freedom of speech. He *did* say 'Ecrasez l'infame' (crush the infamy), urging the overthrow of unfair powers enjoyed by the aristocracy and the superstition and intolerance fostered by the Church.

A spell in the Bastille failed to silence him, and he continued to lead the intellectual charge against the repression which characterized the old order in Europe, supporting the liberating ideas of Newton and Locke. His most famous book, *Candide* (1759), romps through the eighteenth-century disasters of wars and earthquakes, with its irrepressible Doctor Pangloss, a parody of Leibniz, assuring everyone that 'everything is for the best in this best of all possible worlds'. Voltaire himself was sceptical of the Church, being a deist rather than a Christian, and attacked the use of the Bible to repress free thought. 'Those who can make you believe absurdities,' he claimed, 'can make you commit atrocities.'

Like many Enlightenment figures, Voltaire was proficient in many fields, publishing historical and scientific papers in addition to his literary works. He published (anonymously) the *Diction-naire Philosophique* (1764), setting out the case against the fanaticism and repression practiced by the Church, and his admiration of tolerance and free speech. The book itself was condensed and small because he wanted people to carry it around with them as a pocket-sized aid to revolution.

Pervading his thought is the notion that it is important to understand the true reason for things in order to avoid being trapped into superstition. He represented the enquiring and unfettered spirit of the age, with humankind finally breaking from the bonds of darkness and barbarism. He was thus a beacon of hope to the aspiring minds emerging from the straitjacket of ignorance and dogma.

47. Benjamin Franklin
1706–1790

Franklin was the epitome of an eighteenth-century polymath, successfully involved in a range of activities, any one of which could have given him a satisfactory career. He called himself a printer long after he achieved fame in other fields, for it was where he started. When his schooling finished at 10, he was apprenticed as a printer to his brother, and became by turns a publisher and newspaper editor in Philadelphia.

Fame came with his publication of *Poor Richard's Almanack* (from 1733). It was full of useful information about weather and crop management, with the kind of tips and snippets useful to the American colonists taming the wilderness and building homes and lives in a new country. Franklin filled it with home-spun philosophy reflecting his own frugal morality. The almanack sold 10,000 copies a year and made him a rich man.

His affluence enabled him to undertake scientific experiments and invention. He studied electricity, establishing that lightning was electric by flying kites to collect electrical charge from clouds. He never tempted lightning to strike his kites, but others did and were killed. More cautiously, Franklin invented the lightning rod. He also found time to invent bifocal spectacles, the glass harmonica and the efficient metal stove that bears his name.

He never patented his inventions, for the general good and civic virtue came high on the list of the qualities he urged on his fellows. He founded a society which started the first lending library in America, the first fire department, and urged civic improvements. His own Presbyterian upbringing endowed him with a morality whose virtues included thrift, hard work, self-control and a sense of duty, and these were ones he recommended to others. He wanted a democratic citizenship able to sustain itself and prosper, and he rejected authoritarianism, testifying in the British House of Commons against the hated Stamp Act.

He played a key role in securing independence for America, acting as their commissioner to France, trading his agreeable reputation and diplomatic skills to gain their support in the War of Independence. He was one of five who drafted the Declaration of Independence, replacing Jefferson's 'sacred and undeniable' truths by ones that were 'self-evident'.

Franklin combined the scientific, tolerant thinking of the Enlightenment with the moral virtues imparted by a Non-conformist upbringing which progressed into deism. Only a virtuous citizenry could sustain a country and achieve happiness, was his message, and Franklin himself was its exemplar.

48. David Hume
1711–1776

Famed in his day for his best-selling *History of England*, David Hume is now hailed as a highly influential philosopher. He was denied chairs of philosophy in both Edinburgh and Glasgow for his implicit atheism, though he was careful to publish controversial pieces anonymously or posthumously.

Hume's *Treatise on Human Nature* (1739) studied the human mind scientifically, starting with a few simple principles. We have impressions from our senses, says Hume, vivacious and lively, and we have less vivid ideas derived from them. Hume admits no other source of knowledge. He rejects the notion that our mental impressions represent real external objects. We cannot know if they do, he says, since we have no knowledge of real objects to compare them with.

Rather than inquiring about any 'ultimate' reality, Hume's account is naturalistic and non-metaphysical, based on experience and observation. He is sceptical of reason; it is habit, not reason, which leads us to suppose real objects. But scepticism cannot help us live; for practical purposes we suppose that our senses tell us of real things.

His *Treatise* 'fell dead-born from the press', as Hume put it, but he later reworked its ideas into his more successful *Enquiry Concerning Human Understanding* (1748). Hume suggests that induction derives from instinct, not reason, based on our unfounded supposition that what happened yesterday will happen again tomorrow. We project past experience into the future, without a rational link between them.

His account of causality is similar. It is only the 'constant conjunction' of events that leads us to suppose one causes the other; no rational threads connect them to each other. Again, though, in the world beyond the study we assume causality because it helps us.

In his ethics he relegates reason as 'the slave of the passions'. Passion directs us to act, though reason might tell us how. Hume denied morals could be deduced from descriptive statements, for that would involve moving from ones about 'is and is not' to those involving 'ought and ought not' – an unsupported new relationship.

Hume's posthumous *Dialogues Concerning Natural Religion* (1779) opposes the argument from design. We cannot deduce causes from effects, and have only one universe to work on. On seeing a watch we only suppose there is a watchmaker because we have seen watchmakers make watches. We never saw anyone make a universe. In his appended essay on miracles, Hume suggests that the 'folly or knavery' of witnesses is easier to believe than the alleged miracles themselves.

49. Jean-Jacques Rousseau
1712–1778

Jean-Jacques Rousseau's life coincided with the Enlightenment, but his work opposed many of its values, leading some to describe him as counter-Enlightenment, or as an early Romantic.

Swiss born to a mother who died after childbirth and a father who abandoned him, Rousseau's troubled private life included extramarital liaisons, several illegitimate children, and bouts of paranoia. He fell out with everyone who befriended him, even David Hume.

He had written on music for Diderot's *Encyclopedie* when he entered an essay contest on the theme 'Has the restoration of the sciences and arts tended to purify morals?' Rousseau's answer presaged his entire philosophical outlook. His *Discourse on Science and the Arts* (1750) takes the view that the natural goodness of primitive man in a state of nature has been corrupted by civilization.

His essay won, and was followed by his *Discourse on the Origins of Inequality* (1755) and by *The Social Contract* (1762). Following Hobbes and Locke, Rousseau looks beyond society, imagining man in an earlier, primitive state. Rousseau's vision has been called 'the noble savage', depicting early man as free, uncorrupted, peaceable, and driven only by self-preservation and compassion for his fellows. 'Man is born free,' he says, 'but is everywhere in chains.'

Progress in agriculture and early manufactures has enabled humans to store value, bringing private property, inequality and the vices Rousseau sees arising from them, including idleness, luxury and vanity. Arts and sciences divert people from true values such as patriotism, friendship and care for the unfortunate. Rousseau praises ancient Sparta for banning art and literature in favour of military prowess, and condemns Athens for its artistic and intellectual output.

Rousseau regards a return to nature as impossible, so he seeks to move from the corruption of current society towards one which allows for virtuous lives. He favours classical republicanism, with citizens making laws directly, not through representatives. There is tension between the freedom possessed by each individual and the 'general will' for the good of society, and those who do not obey the latter must be 'forced to be free'.

In *Emile* (1762), Rousseau describes the ideal education for a boy; allowed to live like a natural animal until 12, then developing reason, and being taught a skill at age 16. The idea of allowing children to develop naturally was hugely influential on progressive education, though Rousseau abandoned his own children to an orphanage. Rousseau's political views were also influential, cited by many who later participated in the French Revolution.

50. Denis Diderot
1713–1784

Diderot, with Voltaire and Rousseau, was one of the great French intellectuals of the eighteenth-century Enlightenment. Philosophers and writers led a movement, especially in France, against the oppressive authority of aristocracy and clergy. It was to culminate in the French Revolution and the overthrow of the Ancien Régime. Central to Enlightenment thinking was that knowledge and reason could liberate the mind of man, and Diderot's contribution (with D'Alembert) was to collect and publish all information on record in a great *Enclopédie* of 29 volumes, which was to occupy 20 years of his life.

Deciding to become a writer instead of pursuing a career in the Church or in law, Diderot found it difficult to gain recognition or financial security. His first independent work, *Philosophical Thoughts* (1746), was burned by the Parlement of Paris for its anti-Christian implications, but helped to establish his name among Europe's intellectuals. His *Letters on the Blind* (1749) dealt with Locke's view of how our senses affect our ideas, and anticipated teaching blind people to read by touch.

His great work was the *Encyclopédie*. It started as a translation into French of Chambers' *Encyclopedia*, but rapidly took on a life of its own as Diderot persuaded the publisher to turn it into a compendium of all knowledge. It was a political act because it aimed to make self-improvement and social advancement possible in a world still under the thumb of an all-powerful clergy and aristocracy. Its aim was 'to change the common way of thinking' by disseminating knowledge, and in doing so it challenged the grip of those in power. It drew contributions by many of the Enlightenment thinkers of the day, including Voltaire, Jefferson and Franklin.

The authorities were hostile to the project after the first volume appeared in 1751. With the appearance of the second

volume in 1752, the courts suspended the project, but it continued despite them. In 1759 it was formally suppressed, but
went underground. There followed years of harassment and
police raids, but Diderot doggedly continued. It brought him
little financial reward, and it was only through a salary from
Catharine II of Russia and her purchase of his library that Diderot
found any security.

Diderot took the radical view that 'the good of the people
must be the great purpose of government', and used the *Encyclopédie* to promote the Enlightenment ideas of freedom of
thought and expression, and of the importance of science and
industry to the advancement of the human condition.

51. Adam Ferguson
1723–1816

Adam Ferguson belonged to the group of powerful and original Scots thinkers of late eighteenth century who constituted the Scottish Enlightenment. Like his contemporaries David Hume and Adam Smith, Ferguson travelled in Europe and met many of the leading intellectuals of his day. He abandoned his early career as a chaplain to the Black Watch regiment, after fighting in the Battle of Fontenoy, to become a law librarian and then a professor at Edinburgh.

He wrote a history of the fall of Rome in the years before Gibbon's account, and eventually published his lectures on the *Principles of Morals and Political Science*, but it was his *Essay on Civil Society* (1767), published against Hume's advice, that had enduring influence through some of its key insights.

Ferguson is regarded as a founding father of sociology because he treats man as a social creature. He does not speculate about society's origins from any hypothetical 'state of nature', nor does he suppose there was ever a 'social contract'. Instead of such abstract reasoning, Ferguson's account is rooted firmly in actual human experience. 'The forces of society,' he tells us, 'arise before the date of philosophy, from the instincts, not the speculations of men.' Men not only pursue happiness, he observes, but vie for power over others.

Far from achieving harmony through social interaction, says Ferguson, man's relations with his fellows have led to diversity and conflict. And these have helped to drive his progress, which is made socially and culturally, not by any biological inheritance. Many influences help shape him, including those brought about by necessity, or acquired through habit and the influences of family and society.

One of Ferguson's most original observations is that human societies are not planned, but arise spontaneously, 'and nations stumble upon establishments, which are indeed the result of human action, but not the execution of any human design'. This theme of spontaneous order was taken up by Hayek in the twentieth century to set up cultural evolution in opposition to so-called 'scientific socialism'.

But Ferguson also influenced others. His observation that the division of labour led to increased productivity was a precursor to Adam Smith's ideas, and his belief that this would lead to the stratification of society, with repetitive unskilled work degrading those at the lower levels, influenced Marx's thinking. 'The exaltation of a few must depress the many,' was how Ferguson expressed his pessimism about commercial expansion.

52. Adam Smith
1723–1790

Celebrated as the father of modern economics, Adam Smith was famous in his own time as a moral philosopher. Unlike many Enlightenment contemporaries who lived through turbulent times, Smith led a fairly placid life, with his brief childhood kidnap by gypsies ranking as one of its most exciting incidents. He was the archetypal absent-minded professor, putting bread and butter into his teapot, or wandering 15 miles in his nightgown, lost in thought.

His *Theory of Moral Sentiments* (1759) advanced the idea that the most characteristic human trait is 'sympathy' for our fellow beings. The modern word 'empathy' is closer, for Smith's claim is that, from the most exalted to the meanest, we all feel pleasure at another's joy, and sorrow at their grief, simply because we are humans.

We want to be thought to behave properly, but are more indulgent of our own failings than those of others. However, said Smith, we imagine what others think of us, as if there were an 'impartial spectator' in our minds, appraising us more critically than we would ourselves, and this constrains our behaviour.

The book brought Smith celebrity, and an appointment as tutor to the young Duke of Buccleugh, accompanying him around Europe. Smith met Europe's leading intellectuals, observed varieties of industry and commerce, for ten years making notes which became *The Wealth of Nations* (1776). It changed economic thinking.

Others had thought wealth fixed, so countries tried to part with as little of it and to hoard as much of it as possible. Smith countered this by showing how wealth is created, principally by the division of labour and by trade. By specialization into different tasks, a pin-maker who might make 20 pins a day can, with 9 colleagues, produce 48,000. A household can, by buying from specialist bakers and butchers, gain better value than by making everything themselves. The same is true of countries. We could 'by means of hotwalls and glass-houses' grow grapes and make wine on Ben Nevis, but it would cost us less to buy French wine.

We are all self-interested, said Smith – not selfish in any bad sense, but legitimately looking after our interests. We advance them by producing goods and services that others want, and are led 'as if by an invisible hand' to aid others in the process. Smith was sceptical of government since people usually are better at advancing their own interests, and are less likely to waste their own money than are governments.

53. Immanuel Kant
1724–1804

Immanuel Kant spent his life in Köningsberg, mostly at its university, never venturing more than 50 miles away. Nonetheless, his influence has spread across the world, influencing subsequent thinkers. He is said to have effected a 'Copernican revolution in philosophy' by creating a synthesis between empiricism, which holds that knowledge comes only via observation, and rationalism, which takes it to come from deduction based on prior ideas.

Kant's great insight, published in his *Critique of Pure Reason* (1781), is that the human mind is not a blank slate onto which observations pour from outside. Instead, it is an active agent that participates in the acquisition of knowledge by processing the inputs it perceives. This means that our knowledge of the world depends on the structure of our minds. Ideas like space and time do not exist in the universe beyond us; they are our way of interpreting the inputs we receive. 'The matter of our experience is due to our senses,' says Kant, 'and its form is contributed by the mind.'

In addition to statements that are true by definition, and those that can be checked by observation, Kant proposed a third class of synthetic a priori truths, constituting a reality independent of the world of experience, a world of 'things in themselves'. This reality is forever unknown because we can only apprehend things with our mind and senses, limiting our knowledge to the sensory world. Our minds mediate our experiences, and the way we perceive and reflect has a structure governing how we interpret things. The mind does not create the world, but it constitutes the way it appears.

Two things fill Kant with admiration and awe, 'the starry heavens above me and the moral law within me'. He believes that the nature of reality and human morality are both grounded in reason. There is, to Kant, a moral law like the law of nature, and both are compatible because they arise from the way our minds impose order on data.

In his *Groundwork to the Metaphysics of Morals* (1785), Kant identifies the supreme moral law, which he calls the 'categorical imperative'. It is that we should treat everyone as ends in themselves, not a means to someone else's ends. Our own moral behaviour should be only that which we are prepared to see applied as a universal principle.

Kant applied remarkable self-discipline to his own life, with a methodical timetable so exact that people set their watches by his daily walks.

54. Edmund Burke
1729–1797

Edmund Burke is acclaimed as a founder and most eloquent advocate of modern conservatism. Born in Dublin, Burke moved to England and a career in the political events of the late eighteenth century. He never articulated his philosophy in a systematic way, but it permeates his writings and speeches.

In an age when the spirit of enlightenment and reason were abroad, and old traditions were under attack, Burke took the view that there was wisdom enmeshed in society's traditions and practices, and that societies which had endured contained values worthy of respect. 'Many of our men of speculation,' he said, 'instead of exploding general prejudices, employ their sagacity to discover the latent wisdom which prevails in them.'

He supported the American Revolution on pragmatic grounds, seeing it as the defence of established ways against Crown encroachment. His speeches on 'American Taxation' and 'Conciliation with America' urged restraint upon an imperial government asserting its legal powers in what he thought were unwise ways. He saw government not as an assertion of rights but as an exercise in cooperation which should emphasize things that worked rather than constitutional niceties.

His response to the French Revolution was different, and utterly hostile. Here, he thought, men were trying to tear up society and create a new one from abstract principles. His *Reflections on the Revolution in France* was published in 1790, in the early days of general optimism about it. He denounced it, though, predicting it would lead to mayhem and slaughter. His book, denounced for its intemperance, was vindicated somewhat by events as France's Revolution turned to bloodshed, terror and chaos. In contrast with the French intelligentsia, Burke said, 'We are afraid to put men to live and trade each on his own private stock of reason, because we suspect that this stock in each man is small.' Better to draw on the general wisdom of society, he asserted, its past as well as its present.

Burke's book drew a huge reaction, including Thomas Paine's *Rights of Man*, and put an alternative case to the view that society should be based on rational principles rather than inherited traditions. It is a cautious view of progress which has influenced many since. Burke's own political career was unsuccessful, nearly all of it spent in opposition, and dominated by his role in the unsuccessful impeachment of Warren Hastings, first Governor-General of India. His writings, however, provide an eloquent and enduring expression of conservative principles.

55. Thomas Jefferson
   1743–1826

Thomas Jefferson was educated and talented in so many areas that he could have achieved distinction in any one of them. He is remembered as the author of the US Declaration of Independence and its third president, but he typified the enquiring mind of the eighteenth-century Enlightenment. As well as a statesman, he was an architect and an archaeologist, a farmer and horticulturist, an inventor and an author. He was fluent in Latin, Greek and French, and even mastered Scots Gaelic. His home at Monticello shows the flavour of his restless and versatile intellect. President Kennedy, hosting 49 Nobel laureates, called them 'the most extraordinary collection of talent and of human knowledge that has ever been gathered together at the White House — with the possible exception of when Thomas Jefferson dined alone'.

Jefferson's political philosophy rested on liberty, which he based on the natural rights he thought God-given to all. His own religious outlook was a version of the deism prevalent among the intelligentsia of his day. He strongly opposed all religious repression and zealotry, writing in a letter, 'I have sworn upon the altar of god, eternal hostility against every form of tyranny over the mind of man.' He strongly backed the separation of Church and state.

His view of liberty was straightforward. It consisted in doing what one wanted to, provided it did not stop others doing likewise. He viewed governments with suspicion, thinking them more likely to waste people's resources than to help them. Jefferson also distrusted cities and spoke harshly of financiers and bankers; his ideal citizen was an independent yeoman farmer. Like other landowners, he owned slaves himself, despite his dislike of slavery and public moves to limit it.

He named Locke as an influence on his thought, along with Bacon and Newton, and from Locke took the view of government as a contract between people and their rulers. Liberty was a right, not something gifted by government, although governments could destroy it. Governments derived their just powers from the consent of the governed; it was a two-way process. And although law had force to back it, it was often the tyrant's will rather than the expression of justice. Jefferson thought people had an innate sense of morality, separate from law.

Jefferson originally supported the French Revolution and its Declaration of Rights, but deplored its excess of violence and terror, and abhorred its descent into dictatorship.

56. Johann Herder
1744–1803

Johann Herder pioneered the study of the role of language in thought, and developed an innovative philosophy of history. Yet, as a counter-Enlightenment figure who explored the roots of nationalism, he had even more significance and influence.

Herder enrolled in medicine, but found he fainted at every operation or dissection, so switched to theology. He made an empirical study of languages, publishing his influential *Essay on the Origins of Language* (1772), being the first to identify reason with language and to equate thinking with inner speaking. To Herder, language is the origin of reason, guiding our thought. Human children are vulnerable, he suggests, so they can learn language while under adult protection, and with it their culture's values and ways of thinking, making them part of the social group.

Language, says Herder, separates us from the animals; it comes from the soul, not the mouth, and along with poetry, arises from human nature rather than the gift of divine providence. Knowledge is only possible through language. Herder went along with the 'Sturm und Drang' ('storm and stress') literary movement, and taught Germans to glory in their hitherto undervalued language, and to take pride in their origins. 'A poet,' he says, 'is the creator of the nation around him.'

Herder's philosophy of history, expressed in his *Idea for a Philosophy of History of Mankind* (1784–91), sees no general patterns or historical cycles, only the particular character and culture which set the tone of each epoch. For him individual development ascends through family and community into national development, with each nation developing to its own uniquely valuable pattern. Herder dislikes centralism and imperialism because they distort that different development.

He defines nationhood not by political boundaries but by a

common culture, and explores the origins of national identity, including not only its language but its art, music and myths. The Brothers Grimm drew inspiration from him to collect their tales of German folklore, and Herder himself compiled an anthology of folk songs.

Herder rejects the notion that personality is split between reason and feeling, insisting instead that they interact as part of a single nature from which primitive feelings develop into reason. The 'volk' who spring from those shared feelings are not just the common people but the embodiment of the nation, including its aristocracy.

A successful figure at the Weimar court, Herder's ideas influenced the young Goethe, German literature, and the later thinking of Hegel and Nietzsche, as well as the modern study of nationalism.

57. Jeremy Bentham
1748–1832

Bentham went to university at 12, graduating at 16. He qualified in law but never practised it, preferring to write about legal matters instead. He applied rational calculation to the study of ethics, and is recognized as one of the most rigorous of the utilitarians. The doctrine espoused in his *Principles of Morals and Legislation* has little to do with what we now call 'utility' or usefulness. Instead, it treats actions as right or wrong, not on account of the motives that inspire them but in terms of the consequences they produce.

More specifically, Bentham held that an action was good if it brought pleasure, and bad insofar as it brought pain. Actions were better if they brought more pleasure, or pleasure to greater numbers, and the highest good was that which brought the greatest happiness to the greatest number. Bentham called this the 'greatest happiness principle'. He said we should seek the greatest, most widespread balance of pleasure over pain.

We all pursue our own pleasure, said Bentham, but it takes laws to lead us into behaviour which will bring happiness to others and restrain us from infringing their pursuit of their own happiness. He was very democratic about it. The happiness of some groups was not more important than that of others. On the contrary, he wanted 'everybody to count for one, nobody for more than one'.

Nor was he impressed by the notion that some pleasures might be 'higher' or more valuable than others. Not so, he claimed, 'quantity of pleasure being equal, pushpin is as good as poetry'. Critics point out that there are no units to measure happiness, especially in different people, and that under his system the infliction of pain on some would be acceptable if it brought greater pleasure to others. Moreover, his ethics have no place for a sense of justice, yet people feel some things to be wrong even though they might bring greater happiness.

Bentham dismissed the idea of natural rights shared by all. He regarded rights as something endowed by authority through its laws. He declared that, 'Natural rights is simple nonsense: natural and imprescriptible rights, rhetorical nonsense — nonsense upon stilts.'

He is honoured as one of the instigators behind University College London, where his mummified body, fully clothed but with a wax head, sits in a glass case at an entrance, to be brought occasionally to meetings of the College Council.

58. Wilhelm Hegel
   ## 1770–1831

Georg Friedrich Wilhelm Hegel is regarded as the culmination of German idealism in that he constructed a vast philosophical system based on 'spirit', the universal consciousness. His professorial career interrupted by Napoleon's invasion of Jena, Hegel worked as a newspaper editor, then a school head teacher, before settling as a professor in Berlin and drawing admiring students from all over Europe.

Hegel's system supposes that the fundamental structure of reality must be discernible from the structure of our own thought, in that reality itself is rational. Hegel goes on to suppose that the process by which we arrive at logical truths must be the same process by which reality progresses.

In both cases the key is dialectic. Hegel's account, given in *The Phenomenology of Spirit* (1806) and *The Science of Logic* (1812), is that our thought progresses by a three-stage process. Starting with a 'thesis', we are led to contemplate its opposite, the 'antithesis', and from a conflict between the two, a 'synthesis' emerges. This, in turn, provides the new thesis for the next triad. As an example, he suggests that if we contemplate 'being', just the idea itself divorced from any particular thing in being, we find ourselves thinking of no thing, or 'nothing'. Thesis and antithesis can be reconciled in the notion of 'becoming'.

It is not only our logic that progresses through these triads. According to Hegel, history itself is working through similar processes to the self-actualization and self-consciousness of 'the Absolute'. 'The history of the world is none other than the progress of the consciousness of freedom,' he says. Each stage of history constitutes a thesis to be faced by its antithesis, and with a synthesis arising out of their conflict representing a higher stage of development.

Political life began with the family, whose antithesis was civil society without the familial bond, and the synthesis emerging from the conflict was the state. In this manner, history has progressed through conflict, each time reaching a higher stage, and its ultimate goal is that self-awareness of the Absolute.

Popular though it was in drawing together history, philosophy, art and religion, critics pointed out that Hegel took his own day to be the end of history, with the Prussian monarchy as its culmination. He also regarded his own insights as the culmination of philosophy.

Hegel was hugely influential. His dialectic, stripped of 'Spirit', became Marx's dialectical materialism, predicting the inevitable triumph of communism. The Anglo-American tradition, however, with its strict criteria for sense and meaning, made Hegel less influential there than he was on continental thinking.

59. Arthur Schopenhauer
       1788–1860

If Democritus was dubbed the 'laughing philosopher', Schopenhauer easily merits the title 'philosopher of pessimism', in that he paints a gloomy, tortured existence wracked by unsatisfied wants, and relieved only by thinking oneself into non-existence. It's not quite 'life's a bitch, then you die', but it's close.

Schopenhauer's life was unhappy. He entered commerce to please his father, but left it for academe when his father died. He was estranged from his mother, a literary lady with many friends. Schopenhauer apparently had none. He had brief affairs, one of which produced a child who died young. A solitary, unhappy figure, he had a pessimistic temperament which pervaded his philosophy.

He thought his idea of the primacy of will would unite different stands of philosophy and bring him recognition. He arranged his lectures to clash with Hegel's, but found himself facing empty classrooms. He renounced teaching and concentrated on books, chief among which were *The World as Will and Representation* (1818), *On the Will in Nature* (1836), and *Pererga und Paralipomena* (roughly, 'Comments and Omissions') (1851). The last work, a collection of well-written essays and insights, finally brought him recognition and status, perhaps because his pessimism struck a popular mood.

Schopenhauer rejected reason, appealing instead to intuition. Instead of citing evidence and history, his philosophy looks to people's direct experiences of their inner selves. He takes much from Kant, but equates Kant's unknowable 'thing-in-itself' with will, 'the selfsame unchangeable being which is before us'. Will is the reality, says Schopenhauer, of which body is the experience. What we perceive as our body is really will. It is outside space and time, the universal will; only perspective leads someone to interpret their will as separate.

Russell notes that most philosophers would equate this with God, and teach virtue as conformity with it. Schopenhauer does not; he equates it with strife and frustration, and the pain and futility of unachievable goals. Will promises no contentment; and the only pleasure is absence from pain. Schopenhauer's answer lies in Eastern mysticism, seeking the renunciation of desire through nothingness, negating the self through contemplation.

Schopenhauer himself never renounced desire. He enjoyed good food and dallied in sexual liaisons. He had a fierce temper, and when he injured an aged seamstress by throwing her downstairs, had to make support payments thereafter. When she died 20 years later he wrote on the death certificate an elegant but heartless pun, 'Obit anus, abit onus' (the old woman dies, the burden departs).

60. Mary Shelley
1797–1851

Mary Wollstonecraft Shelley lived a life shockingly unconventional by the standards of her day. Unlike most women of her time, she was a free spirit who came to exemplify the yearning of women to break free of restricting conformity and to live independent lives. Her mother, the feminist Mary Wollstonecraft, died giving birth to her, but the daughter was influenced by her late mother's works.

Her eccentric upbringing included meeting some leading literary and scientific figures of the day in her father, William Godwin's, house. These included Lord Byron, Wiliam Blake and Percy Bysshe Shelley, with whom she fell in love at 16, eloped, and bore an illegitimate daughter who died in infancy. She married Shelley after his own wife committed suicide.

At a celebrated house party in Switzerland she was challenged by Lord Byron to write a ghost story. Her response was *Frankenstein: or, The Modern Prometheus* (1818), which started as a short story but expanded into a novel. Its powerful theme and vivid writing made it a huge success. Prometheus, who brought men fire from the gods, finds his echo in the aristocrat Viktor Frankenstein, who defies God's creation of life by applying science to make his own. The body parts garnered from butcher's shops and mortuaries are assembled and given the spark of life. Mary Shelley had seen experiments in galvanism conducted by Sir Humphrey Davy in her father's house. Her monster, though repulsive, was intelligent and articulate, but turned to evil. Frankenstein himself dies confronting it in the snowy wilderness.

Although some have seen a parable of childbirth in the story, its chief power lies in its rejection of the optimism of the Enlightenment. The supposition that advances in knowledge bring improvements to the human condition is countered by a dark, romantic tale of gothic horror. Its settings and characters echo the late oppressors from which humankind had been recently liberated, and in the story scientific knowledge brings grief through its hubris.

Mary Shelley wrote other novels, though none as famous as *Frankenstein*. Her apocalyptic story *The Last Man* (1826) antici-pates modern disaster stories by telling of a virulent plague which wipes out humanity. Her own life was marred by tragedy: three children died in infancy, and her husband Shelley drowned in a boating accident when she was only 25. Shunned by the social circles of her day, she nonetheless established a reputation in her own right, having penned the novel whose theme has been reworked in so many motion pictures.

61. Auguste Comte
      1798–1857

Among Auguste Comte's legacies are the word 'sociology' in its modern meaning, and the philosophical approach called 'positivism'. Comte himself, born in the aftermath of the French Revolution, sought a new order to explain the modern world, one that would point the way to mankind's future. He sought a scientific account of human social behaviour to parallel the laws which Newton had formulated for the physical sciences.

Although he was inspired by Condorcet's optimistic view of human progress, Comte's own life was unhappy. Even while writing his six-volume *Course of Positive Philosophy* (1830–42), he suffered mental illnesses and was several times in mental institutions.

He traced human development through three historical phases. Before the Enlightenment had come the 'Age of Theology', in which people supposed nature had a will of its own and were governed by unthinking belief and superstition. Then the 'Age of Metaphysics' had come with the French Revolution, putting abstract ideas such as universal rights in place of the old beliefs. Finally had come the 'Scientific Age', in which people came to understand the physical laws by which the world was governed.

Comte's positivism took the view that true knowledge only came from rational consideration of sense experiences, and this was how science had progressed. He divided the sciences into three groups: there were the inorganic ones such as astronomy and physics, the organic ones such as biology, and finally the social sciences. It was in the third group that he called for an 'urgently needed reorganization of politics, ethics, and religion'.

He synthesized intellectual developments in different disciplines into an overall interpretation of history and progress. Social statics, he said, described the forces that held societies together, while social dynamics dealt with social change. Comte himself was inspired by the need for change to a more rational and scientific order, though his positivism increasingly took the form of a new, secular religion whose hierarchical structure mirrored that of the Catholic Church. In his political vision, society's education and morality would be determined by social scientists, whereas businessmen and bankers would run its economy. Democracy, he thought, would only lead to the rule of ignorance rather than knowledge.

The modern world, which has witnessed several attempts to impose rational scientific order, is perhaps less sympathetic to Comte's vision than his successors were. Although he died in obscurity, positivism proved widely influential for many decades, and Comte's saying 'Order and Progress' even adorns the modern flag of Brazil.

62. Frédéric Bastiat
1801–1850

Frédéric Bastiat was an innovative figure in political and economic philosophy. His support for individual liberties combined with free markets and free trade made him an early advocate of modern libertarianism. His boyhood was spent under Napoleon's Continental System which restricted trade for strategic reasons, and Bastiat experienced the effects of tariffs and regulation when he left school to enter his family's business.

Inheriting his grandfather's estate at 25, Bastiat became a gentleman farmer, handing over its management to others in order to spend his life as a writer and thinker. The case he put in essays and pamphlets was that government was untrustworthy, inefficient, a bad economic manager, and too easily captured by organized producer interests, at cost to the consumer. It is, he said, 'the great fiction through which everybody endeavours to live at the expense of everybody else'.

Governments were there, said Bastiat, to defend life, liberty and property. 'These three gifts from God precede all human legislation,' he said, 'and are superior to it.' People were motivated by self-interest, not selfishly but benignly because the free market brought 'economic harmony' among people; and his views on the market's function to coordinate activity by different participants are regarded as a precursor to the Austrian School of economics. He developed innovative ideas, including the notion that value is subjective, established by voluntary exchange.

His first article mocked merchants who demanded that tariffs in agriculture be abolished while those on manufactures be retained. Mockery and satire were his weapons. His *Economic Sophisms* (1845) contains an appeal by the French candle-makers demanding government to shut out unfair competition from the sun. He founded the Free Trade Association and wrote regularly in its weekly newspaper, gaining a huge popular audience.

Another work called for everyone's right hand to be cut off in order to generate extra work. In another he pointed out that a railway linking France and Spain would have manufacturers in both countries demanding tariffs against imports. Better for governments to destroy all railways, he suggested mischievously. His serious case was that tariffs undermine the benefits that progress and technology achieve. Bastiat urged governments to anticipate the wider consequences as well as the immediate effects of their actions, looking at unseen disadvantages for the many, as well as visible benefits for a few.

He was elected to the 1848 Legislative Assembly, but died of tuberculosis in 1850, the year in which *The Law* was published, setting out the laws of a free society.

63. Ludwig Feuerbach
1804–1872

Although he originally contemplated an ecclesiastical career, Feuerbach became a lifelong critic of religion, and wrote a hugely influential analysis of it. As a young man, Feuerbach joined the radicals inspired by Hegel, and became a leading light in the Young Hegelians. Taking Hegel's view that history was marching to its conclusion and fulfilment, they thought the nineteenth-century institutions and ideas were destined to be swept away. Feuerbach concentrated on Christianity in particular.

His *Thoughts on Death and Immortality* (1830) had expressed Spinoza's view that humans had no personal immortality of the soul, but would only become part of universal nature. Although Feuerbach published it anonymously, people knew he had written it. It ended any hope of an academic career, and Feuerbach became a philosopher and writer supported by the income from his wife's porcelain factory.

His *Essence of Christianity* (1841) was a sensation. It inspired radical youth in Europe and helped form Karl Marx's views on religion, among others. Feuerbach repudiated Hegel's view on the primacy of thought and ideas, and said instead that our knowledge comes from sense experiences and from science. Since our senses have given us no evidence of God, our concept of him must have come from our human situation. Never having met an infinitely powerful and loving being, our idea of God's qualities must be based on human power and love.

What men do, said Feuerbach, is to project their own yearning for perfection into an imaginary being. God represents the highest, but unachieved, human qualities. He is the outward projection of man's inner nature, the realization of human aspirations into a single perfect being. Man makes God in the image of what he yearns to be, thus God is 'an inexpressible sigh deep in the soul of man'.

Not only is God a product of human wishful thinking, said Feuerbach, but he limits and stunts human development by diverting attention away from our fellow men. If men realized that they compensate for earthly failings by imagining super-natural fulfilment, they would concentrate on achievement in this life instead of indulging in fantasies. Men think that justice will be done in heaven, and therefore tolerate injustice in this world. If social conditions were improved, there would be less need for religious illusions, he said, declaring 'Let politics be our religion.'

This rallying cry laid the foundation for the Marxist view of Christianity as a tool of the oppressor classes, and of religion as a diversion from the earthly reforms that were needed.

64. John Stuart Mill
   1806–1873

John Stuart Mill was taught intensively by his father to be the future champion of utilitarian philosophy. It was successful, for Mill became Britain's most eminent and influential nineteenth-century philosopher. Young Mill was taught Greek at 3, Latin at 8, and had read most classical authors by 10. It was not without a price, and Mill later wrote wistfully, 'I never was a boy.' After a nervous breakdown at 20, he found Wordsworth's poetry aided his recovery, and achieved a balance between his intellectual and emotional sides.

Mill set English empiricism against the prevailing German intuitionism. Truths must be gained and tested by experiences of the world outside the mind, he insisted in his *System of Logic* (1843). Trying to derive them from inner intuitions would only consecrate deep-seated prejudices, he said.

The same concern underlies his *Utilitarianism* (1863), as he insists on an external standard of good and right. In the utilitarian tradition of Bentham, a childhood mentor, he equates good with greatest happiness. Unlike Bentham, Mill distinguishes between lower pleasures and more elevated ones, pointing out that those who have knowledge of both invariably choose the latter. 'Better to be a human being dissatisfied than a pig satisfied; better to be Socrates dissatisfied than a fool satisfied,' he says. Critics have claimed that choosing between qualities of pleasure implies some standard other than quantity.

Mill's *On Liberty* (1859) became an enduring classic of libertarianism. It asserts that the only legitimate use of power is to prevent harm to others. This alone justifies restraining a person's freedom of action, whereas 'his own good, either physical or moral, is not sufficient warrant'. It is not enough that behaviour offends; it must bring physical harm or serious risk of it to justify restraints.

Mill's support for individual liberty is not derived from abstract rights but from its consequences. It allows people to develop their individuality, and for society to gain accordingly. If each pursues their own happiness, then together they will pursue the general good of society. The majority must not tyrannize dissenters.

Arguing passionately for liberty, Mill says that it is the plurality of paths which results that has given Europe 'its progressive and many-sided development'. He argues for free speech because the silenced opinion might be correct, and because debate forces people to examine their convictions. It is, he says, a prerequisite for progress.

Mill's principles supported an agenda that led to the political and social reforms which characterized nineteenth-century Britain.

65. Harriet Taylor Mill
1807–1857

Harriet Taylor's published works were few, and by themselves would have made her a significant, but not a major, figure in key areas. Her partnership with John Stuart Mill, however, and her participation in his work have earned her a larger place for her influence and involvement.

At a time when women were expected to conform to domestic roles, she advocated measures to enfranchise them and give them independence. Brought up by Unitarian parents, she married John Taylor at 18 and regretted it. Four years later she met John Stuart Mill, and the two formed a bond which endured throughout her life, and included marriage to him for her last seven years, following the death of her first husband.

In essays under her own name she set out feminist principles and arguments well ahead of their time, arguing that male dominance in the home stunted the development of women, depriving them of incentive and opportunities for education and development. Similar lack of political power trapped them in a servile situation under laws designed to maintain male dominance.

Her essay *The Enfranchisement of Women* (1851) was published under John Stuart Mill's name, but he acknowledged her authorship. It called, radically, for women's suffrage, entitlement to office, and equality in law with men. She analysed the corrosive effect of male dominance on both sexes and on society.

Mill's *Principles of Political Economy* (1848) had a chapter attributed to her 'On the Probable Future of the Labouring Classes', which stresses the importance of universal education, and argues that workers will ultimately seek part-ownership instead of mere wages. This reflects her support for early experiments in collectivism like those of industrialist Robert Owen.

The extent of her contribution to Mill's other works is still controversial. While Mill himself wrote that they shared views and that it mattered little 'which of them holds the pen', some critics have suggested that he praised her more than contemporaries thought justified. His classic *On Liberty* (1859) is dedicated to Harriet, and he wrote, 'Like all that I have written for many years, it belongs as much to her as to me.' Few suppose, however, that she actually wrote any of the words herself.

It was a remarkable intellectual partnership, and she undoubtedly contributed greatly to the ideas developed and expounded by Mill, and won his support for some of her own views. In an age where women had to struggle for serious attention, Harriet Taylor Mill managed to contribute to the development of ideas.

66. Charles Darwin
1809–1882

Darwin completed the removal of humankind from its central position in the universe. Copernicus had moved the earth from the centre, while Newton had shown that heavens and earth obeyed the same laws. Now Darwin showed that humans were not separate from animals; they *were* animals.

Interested in nature since boyhood, Darwin neglected his Edinburgh medical studies to work on anatomy and plant classification. In 1831, the year of his Cambridge degree, came the chance to accompany Captain Robert Fitzroy on the five-year voyage round the world of HMS *Beagle*, and to study life in different habitats.

During the voyage Darwin catalogued and classified, occasionally sending home specimens and notes. He observed, especially in the Galapagos Islands, how animals and birds differed from their mainland counterparts, and between different islands. There were 14 different species of finch among the islands. He knew that Lyell's *Principles of Geology* had pointed to fossils seemingly thousands of millions of years old, and wondered how some species had replaced others.

Back in England, Darwin read the gloomy verdict of Malthus that animals always reproduce more than the environment can sustain. Wondering which ones survived, Darwin finally understood that individuals with an advantage, even a slight one, would survive preferentially to breed and pass it to their offspring. He spent 20 years developing the idea and documenting evidence for it, writing notes in 1844 for publication if he died.

In 1858 a paper arrived from Alfred Russell Wallace, who had developed the same idea, also after reading Malthus. Joint presentation of papers was agreed, and in 1859 *The Origin of Species* was published, selling out immediately. While Darwin did not say in it that humans had evolved from earlier creatures, he did say,

'Light will be thrown on the origin of man,' and went on to publish *The Descent of Man* (1871).

Darwin had provided the mechanism by which species replace each other. In place of a world made suddenly with its myriad life forms, Darwin substituted one which had developed over millions of years according to readily understood processes. Variation and natural selection, later combined with Mendel's genetics, make humans a natural developing part of the universe.

The theory of evolution importantly proposed a new mechanism of change. In place of sudden, perhaps violent, substitution of one state for another, Darwin showed how change could occur incrementally over time, with one gradually replacing the other. Evolution is seen at work in other areas, including economics and society.

67. Pierre-Joseph Proudhon
1809–1865

Pierre-Joseph Proudhon was the most celebrated thinker of the nineteenth-century left, more widely acclaimed than Marx, yet unlike most others, came from peasant stock. As a boy he herded cows, and was only enrolled in his town school when the fees were waived. He was punished for not bringing his books to school; he could not afford any, and borrowed them from friends.

He went into printing and taught himself Latin, Greek and Hebrew from the books he worked on. But it was when he went to Paris in 1839 that he was immersed in its prevailing left-wing ideas, and shaped his own thoughts.

He was the first to call himself an anarchist, and to Proudhon it meant society without a ruler. Men had an absolute right to liberty. He asked *What is Property?* (1840), famously answering that 'property is theft'. He equated property with labour; only what people produced was their property. Capitalists and land-lords therefore 'stole' the proceeds of the labour of others.

Proudhon's anarchy opposed not merely state rule, but that of capitalists and clerics as well. All were sources of unwarranted oppression. 'What capitalism does to labour, and the state to liberty, the Church does to the spirit.' Their joint oppression of the people 'enslaved its body, its will and its reason'.

Rejecting socialist and communist calls for state ownership, Proudhon advocated no ownership except by people over what they produced. Rather than give society power by vesting it with land and the means of production, Proudhon opted for 'user-ownership', with farm workers and artisans possessing their homes and the tools of their trade. It was effectively small-scale ownership, and the system to sustain this he called 'mutualism'.

He rejected Marx's call for revolutionary violence, believing it would 'seriously compromise' social change that should come peacefully. Workers should acquire the means of production through labour associations, and peasants the land, with co-operative bodies trading with each other. A federation of such free communes should replace the state, he argued, in proposals that strongly influenced Bakunin. His *Philosophy of Poverty* (1846) drew the counterblast *Poverty of Philosophy* from Marx who thought him hopelessly naïve.

His proposals reflect his background, in that Proudhon favoured the small scale, peasants and artisans, rather than the industrial societies beginning to dominate, and on which Marx focused his attention.

Proudhon wrote in polemical style for four newspapers, tried and failed to establish a 'People's Bank', but was elected to the 1848 Legislative Assembly.

68. Søren Kierkegaard
1813–1855

Søren Kierkegaard was the father of existentialism. He was also an archetype of the tortured, self-doubting thinker racked by guilt. His wealthy father encouraged his child's imagination by fantasy games, but was himself gloomy and guilt-ridden, shocking his son with his confessions.

Kierkegaard studied theology at first, but turned to philosophy and literature. His writing, much of it written in bursts of passionate intensity, often criticized Hegel and the view that life was explicable on an intellectual level. On the contrary, wrote Kierkegaard, it must be experienced and understood only as it is lived by each individual: 'Life is not a problem to be solved, but a reality to be experienced.'

Sometimes posing as a casual hedonist, Kierkegaard concealed an inner melancholy which permeates his books. He wrote many under pseudonyms, not to conceal his identity, for everyone knew he had written them, but to emphasize different ways of living.

In *Either/Or* (1843) he contrasts two levels of living: the aesthetic and the ethical (and later added a third, the religious). The aesthetic life centres on temporal pleasures, sensory, intellectual and physical. The ethical life centres on morality and the eternal. When someone understands that the aesthetic way leads to dread and despair, they might choose the ethical way.

The 'dread' he writes of in *The Concept of Anxiety* (1844) is at the heart of existentialism. It is the angst one experiences at the thought of one's freedom to choose and the responsibility that accompanies it. It is necessary before the 'leap of faith' can lead someone to the ethical and religious ways. Kierkegaard thinks there is no evidence proving God's existence; indeed, Christianity contains paradoxes and seems incomprehensible and absurd to humans. Only a leap of faith, such as that made by

Abraham offering to sacrifice his son Isaac, can lead one to religious conviction and unconditional obedience to God's will.

In the improbably titled *Concluding Unscientific Postscript to Philosophical Fragments* (1846), Kierkegaard attacks the Hegelian idea of a 'science of the spirit'. Existence cannot be described logically or objectively, he writes, and the truth about one's life is not found conceptually; it is a *chosen* truth. Where Hegel had written, 'the real is rational, the rational is real', Kierkegaard writes, 'subjectivity is truth, truth is subjectivity'.

Believing that the highest task of human existence is to become oneself, he wrote, 'The thing is to find a truth which is true for me, to find the idea for which I can live and die.'

69. Mikhail Bakunin
1814–1876

Mikhail Bakunin sometimes seems like an all-purpose, roving revolutionary of the nineteenth century. There was hardly a revolution he did not participate in or support, including those in Dresden, Prague, Italy and the Paris Commune. Bakunin himself was an anarchist, perhaps its most prominent theorist, and opposed all governments.

Born of a Russian landowner, Bakunin resigned his army commission at age 21 to study philosophy, and became part of a pan-European movement of intellectuals seeking to overthrow the established order of authoritarian governments, a class-based social order, and a capitalist economic system. It is hardly surprising that when the Tsar's agents finally seized him, he spent ten years in Russian prisons and Siberian labour camps before escaping through America to Europe.

Of his published works, he is best known for two written in the last six years of his life: *Statism and Anarchy* (1873) and *God and the State* (1871). In them he expounds his rejection of every form of authority except 'those determined by our own individual nature'. Significantly, this included interim socialist governments. Although Bakunin joined the First International, dedicated to replacing capitalism by socialism, he was in public dispute with another of its leading adherents, Karl Marx. Bakunin rejected Marx's 'dictatorship of the proletariat' as another form of tyranny. 'If you took the most ardent revolutionary,' he said, 'vested him with absolute power, within a year he would be worse than the Tsar himself.'

The alternative propounded by Bakunin was that workers would take over the factories and tools, while the peasants would take over the land. They would rule through voluntary associations, freely cooperating with each other, as they saw fit. This would apply at every level in a kind of voluntary federalism.

People would work together to secure equal education for children and equal chances for people to work to better their lives.

This vision influenced young people across Europe with its optimistic view of human nature, but was criticized as naïve, lacking the mechanisms by which power might be seized and held. Bakunin himself opposed the leadership of the intelligentsia. Any 'enlightened elite' could only influence the masses, and must have no power itself, he said, or it would seek to perpetuate its power by keeping people dependent.

Bakunin opposed every outside authority from God downwards, and considered liberty 'the unique condition under which intelligence, dignity and human happiness can develop and grow'. He said, 'where the state begins, individual liberty ceases, and vice versa'.

70. Karl Marx
1818–1883

Karl Marx was historically important as the inspiration behind Lenin's Bolshevik Revolution of 1917 and the establishment of the Russian communist state. He was a founding father of communism, co-authoring *The Communist Manifesto* (1848) with Friedrich Engels. Settling in Britain at age 30, he later wrote *Das Kapital* (1867), famously researched in the reading room of the British Museum.

He regarded human history as the story of class conflict, and thought it would reach its conclusion in a classless society. He held that social and political change take place as a result of economic change, specifically changes in the technology of production, saying, 'The hand-mill gives you society with the feudal lord; the steam-mill, society with the industrial capitalist.'

Marx took Hegel's theory of change, arguing that each stage of society created the forces that would destroy it, with a new status quo coming from a clash between them. In Marx's view, therefore, historical progress is made in jumps resulting from economic development, and driven by revolutionary violence.

Although Marx approved of Darwin, he failed to embrace Darwin's notion that change can take place through steady variations, with one stage turning gradually into another instead of by violent conflict. Many historical changes seem to have evolved by steady progress rather than sudden upheavals. Critics have also pointed out that if a classless, communist society followed the final stage of capitalism, it should have happened in the most mature economies, rather than in the less advanced economies of Russia and China.

Marx railed against the apparent injustices of nineteenth-century capitalism, the oppression of workers, and the alienation brought about by repetitive mass production. He said that value derived from the labour it took to produce something, and that any profit above that represented 'surplus value', or exploitation by capitalists of the workers who produced it.

He regarded religion as an aid to exploitation. He thought it a human construct to right the world's wrongs in a mythical afterlife. He called religion 'the opium of the people' because instead of campaigning for reform, people were diverted by religion into accepting injustice in this life in return for heavenly recompense.

The demise of communism has diminished Marx's political significance, but the idea that historical change has economic roots is a powerful tool, taken up by many historians who reject the political aspects of Marxism, even though few take it to be the sole explanation of historical events.

71. Herbert Spencer
1830–1903

Herbert Spencer reached a theory of evolution seven years before Darwin published his *Origin of Species*, and it is he, not Darwin, who coined the expression 'the survival of the fittest'. There were, however, fundamental differences. Spencer's evolution lacked the idea of natural selection to describe its mechanism. Indeed, Spencer favoured Lamarckism, in which acquired characteristics could be passed on through the generations.

The other major difference was that Spencer's theory was much wider in scope, featuring evolution in the physical and biological worlds, and also in the psychological and cultural domains. Spencer thought that all these areas were subject to natural laws capable of being known and understood. His own *Principles of Psychology* (1855) sought to discern them in psychology.

Educated by his father and through his own reading, Spencer had worked first as a railway civil engineer, and then on the *Economist* financial magazine. He was a convinced free trader and utilitarian, both of which outlooks he wove into his view of human evolutionary progress. He thought that societies had evolved from simple, hierarchic, militant ones into complex cooperative industrial ones, and that progress occurred because some features were more conducive than others to stability and prosperity. In particular, he thought that the 'liberty of each, limited by the like liberty of all, is the rule in conformity with which society must be organized'.

He elevated this 'liberty principle' to a prime position, backing laissez-faire and freedom of contract, and opposing regulation of business and commerce, preferring limited government instead. Societies which permitted experiment would evolve more benignly and rapidly, and evolution would reach an end point, said Spencer, in 'the perfect man in the perfect society'. This contrasted with Darwin, who saw evolution as a process with no end point at all.

Spencer thought that human beings were evolving into less aggressive creatures as society evolved to diminish aggression's value and to increase that of cooperation. Despite this, the term 'Social Darwinism' was applied to his ideas, as if society were a jungle in which only the fittest could survive. Widely read and distinguished in his day, he had a huge following in the US, where his ideas on individual self-improvement appealed to its aspirational ethic. Even so, his name subsequently came to be associated with hard-hearted and unsympathetic social views. This might have owed something to such pithy expressions as, 'The ultimate effect of shielding men from the effects of folly, is to fill the world with fools.'

72. Charles Peirce
1839–1914

Charles Peirce (pronounced 'purse') was, according to Russell, 'the greatest American thinker ever', and hailed by Popper as 'one of the greatest philosophers of all times'. Yet he enjoyed little celebrity in his day and spent his final years in abject poverty, dependent on charity from friends.

Peirce had a scientific career, though his real love was logic; a taste acquired at age 12 when his father, a Harvard mathematics professor, set him problems to solve. He was Harvard's first MSc in chemistry, but his working career was with the US Coast and Geodetic Survey. He was briefly a logic professor at Johns Hopkins, then blacklisted for his unmarried liaison with a French gypsy. Peirce equated logic with semiotics, the theory of signs, and was among its pioneers.

His contribution to philosophy was made through papers published in journals, and through boxes of unpublished papers only edited and published many years after his death. He treated philosophy as an experimental science, holding that the roots of logic lay not in Cartesian introspection, but in the experience of an objective world. He is, with James and Dewey, a founder of the philosophy of pragmatism, and both the others acknowledge his influence on their thinking.

Pragmatism's origins are in two of his papers, *The Fixation of Belief* (1877) and *How to Make Our Ideas Clear* (1878). Peirce holds that all truths are provisional, and probable rather than certain. He broke new ground with his frequency theory of probability to validate induction.

A theory's truth (and meaning) is bound up with its consequences. Science explains its ideas based on their effects and how we use them; 'Our idea of everything is our idea of its sensible effects,' he writes. Those theories are nearer the truth which outperform their rivals in enabling us to predict (and control) our world. To deduction and induction he adds 'abduction', the provisional acceptance of a theory to explain otherwise surprising facts.

Science is characterized, says Peirce, by 'fallibilism', which admits uncertainty. Belief in absolute certainty is a barrier to enquiry, along with the belief that things are unknowable or inexplicable, or that exactness can be achieved. He describes beliefs as 'habits of action', saying that logic can lead us to sound beliefs. These are not objective certainties, for he admits none; 'the opinion which is fated to be ultimately agreed by all who investigate is what we mean by the truth', and this depends on its conceivable consequences and their uses.

73. William James
1842–1910

William James was instrumental in defining the modern study of psychology. It was a disparate set of observations and insights until he published *Principles of Psychology* (1890). The 1200-page work, which took him 12 years to write, set out the systematic principles which laid the groundwork of the modern discipline. His approach was called 'functionalist', in that it looks on mental activity as a process, to be seen in action, rather than as something whose structure can be examined.

James takes a parallel approach in his philosophy, espousing pragmatism. Instead of seeking eternal objective truths which might exist independently of humankind, he declares truth to be that which is useful to people. At the heart of his epistemology are the needs of human beings, rather than any external reality. 'Every way of classifying a thing is but a way of handling it for some particular purpose,' he wrote. James was a relativist, in that what worked for some people might not work for others: 'Truth is whatever is expedient to our way of thinking.' He talks of the 'cash value' of an idea, meaning its usefulness to us, and takes the Darwinian view that the ultimate test of an idea's usefulness is survivability.

In his life, James constantly suffered from a series of real or imagined ailments, never enjoying rugged health. He was prone to depression, and dabbled in spiritualism and the paranormal, founding the US branch of the Society for Psychical Research. His relativism extends into religion, where he takes the institutions of religion as less significant than people's experiences of it. His Gifford Lectures, published as *The Varieties of Religious Experience* (1902), look at the experiences that different religions have brought to people, and treats religion the way ordinary people take it, as something useful to their lives.

His ideas on emotions are encapsulated in the James-Lange

theory of emotion, which says in its famous example that we do not see a bear, fear it and therefore run; rather, we see a bear, experience the effects of accelerated heart-rate, perspiration and muscular response, and run instinctively – consequently we fear it. Emotion is how these physical stimuli appear to us.

Consciousness, says James, is not a succession of ideas, but has more of the character of a continuous stream. 'In talking of it hereafter, let us call it the stream of thought, of consciousness,' he said, giving birth to the phrase that influenced a generation.

74. Friedrich Nietzsche
1844–1900

Friedrich Nietzsche does not, like conventional philosophers, provide chains of argument leading to his conclusions. Instead his bold assertions invite readers to share his sweeping insights and interpretation. 'Leaping from mountain-top to mountain-top' is his description of it.

Although brought up a devout Lutheran Christian by his pastor father, Nietzsce rejected religion after school, and spent his energy attacking what he called the 'corrupting' influence of religion, especially Christianity.

Christianity has brought, he says, a 'slave morality' to Europe. It represents the efforts of the underclass of slaves and the weak to subdue the natural instincts of the strong and powerful, characterized by a will to power and domination.

In *The Birth of Tragedy* (1872) Nietzsche treats two elements in ancient Greece: Dionysius, representing primal passions, and Apollo, characterized by order and reason. He regrets the triumph of the latter, urging the freeing of suppressed passion. He admires the Homeric qualities of strength, power and bravery in combat.

Crucially, Nietzsche thinks that modern man faces a crossroads reached by the rise of science and secular reasoning and the decline of religion. 'God is dead,' he declares, and a new basis of morality is needed or Europe will sink into nihilism. Without the universal perspective of a ruling god, we each have our own perspectives, and must pursue our own values, with ethics based on human life, not divine revelation.

He published *Thus Spoke Zarathustra* (1883) and *Beyond Good and Evil* (1886), advocating a new 'heroic' morality based on guilt-free self-assertion, and glorying in life's values. The will to power characterizes Nietzsche's 'Superman', the strong one who has broken free, mastered his own passions and turned his energy into passionate creativity. He reaches beyond conventional good and evil, marked out from the 'common herd' by his will to power. In place of an illusory afterlife, he so exults in this life that even if compelled to repeat it eternally, he would joyfully embrace it.

Nietzsche rejects democracy, 'bourgeois' values, and both Kantian and utilitarian ethics. Happiness and 'the good' are deemed unworthy goals, lacking the life-affirming qualities of power, wealth, strength and health. The strong should break free and assert their power and vitality, rejecting the Christian morality which calls their natural inclinations evil.

Nietsche himself had poor health throughout his adult life, with insanity marking his final years. His ideas proved influential in art and poetry as well as philosophy, though the Nazis corrupted his 'strong individual' into advocacy of a master race.

75. John Dewey
1859–1952

John Dewey achieved eminence in philosophy, psychology and education, applying a unity of approach in all three fields. Dewey's concern was to view things not as static but as part of a *process*, a process that defined them. In all three fields he stressed the role of interaction and feedback.

Dewey, along with Peirce and James, was an exponent of the 'pragmatic' school of philosophy, emphasizing the functional aspects of knowledge in serving human purposes. He regarded as unhelpful the separation of mind and matter, as though the world were passively perceived. The two interact, he said, and our contact with the world is processed through our sensations and ideas.

He saw parallels to Darwinism, and regarded the development of knowledge as a human response to its environment, an adaptive one that enables people to survive and to thrive. The mind does not passively soak up knowledge; it interacts with its environment and subjects its ideas to experiment and adaptation. Dewey called his philosophy 'instrumentalism', and used the term 'transactional' to describe a process which does not refer to an ultimate reality or to the 'essences' of things.

In psychology, he challenged the notion of a stimulus eliciting a response. The two are more interwoven, he said, not separate events, and they reinforce each other. Again, his theme is of process and interaction.

Dewey's educational ideas were controversial. He put them into practice from 1896 through his University of Chicago Laboratory Schools. Here, too, he insisted that education does not consist of an authority imparting knowledge to a student, but is instead an experiential process with the student participating and interacting. Dewey thought education essential for a healthy democracy, and his ideas influenced what was termed 'progressive' education in the US, drawing criticism from supporters of more traditional educational methods.

In aesthetics, too, Dewey pointed to the interaction between artistic works and their local culture. While the actual painting or sculpture is an 'art object', it is not of itself a work of art. For that there must be an interaction between the object and its audience.

Dewey opposed Hobbes' view of individuals combining in social contracts, maintaining instead that man is inherently social, and that his mind is social in nature from its very beginning. Humans interact in society and progress thereby, he said. Dewey involved himself in public affairs, was active in social issues, and helped to found the National Association for the Advancement of Colored People (NAACP). He wrote in defence of democracy, in opposition to fascism, and was a vigorous proponent of academic freedom.

76. Edmund Husserl
1859–1938

Edmund Husserl was born of Jewish parents in part of the Austro-Hungarian Empire which now lies within the Czech Republic. He tried early on to synthesize mathematics, psychology and philosophy into our understanding of mathematics, attempting to account for our concept of number. Frege attacked this account for an over-reliance on psychology, claiming this introduced subjectivity everywhere.

Husserl himself realized the problem of trying to move from subjective psychological experiences to certain truths, or basing permanent laws of logic on unreliable mental processes. In subsequent accounts he modified his approach to overcome the difficulty.

Husserl pioneered the philosophy called phenomenology, which deals not with the essences of things as they are in some 'real' external world but concentrates its study instead on how things are perceived. It is the study of things as they appear in our experience (the phemonena). Whether what is behind the phenomena has any objective reality is not important in phenomenology; it seeks to study the conscious experiences themselves and to analyze the mental structures involved in perceiving particular types of object.

The difference between mental phenomena and physical objects, said Husserl, is that the former have 'intentionality', that is, they are directed at something, whereas physical objects are not. Every mental phenomenon refers to an object, and every belief or desire has to be *about* something.

Objects should not be regarded as existing externally, emitting energy that enables us to identify and evaluate them. Rather, they are a collection of aspects we are conscious of which enable us to classify them. And because phenomena are different from physical objects, consciousness must be studied by different methods. Husserl was concerned to distinguish between our consciousness and the object it is directed towards. The 'natural attitude' says that objects have real existence and have a nature we can determine through sensory perception, but the question of real existence must be suspended, says Husserl, so we can concentrate on meanings that are in the mind.

Husserl was not an idealist; he did not deny the reality of external objects. They are real, he said, but are not what they were because of some unique essence they possess but rather because of a relationship between them and an observer perceiving them. Because we concentrate on their meaning in the mind, said Husserl, we must set aside, or 'bracket', the issue of their independent existence.

Phenomenology had an important impact on continental philosophy. It influenced the ideas of several subsequent thinkers, notably Heidegger and Jean-Paul Sartre.

77. Max Weber
   1864–1920

Max Weber is regarded as one of the fathers of modern sociology. He looked in particular at the way in which different religions have affected the societies in which they thrived. Weber studied the religions of ancient China and India and also Judaism to see how religious practices might have influenced economic activity. He conjectured that religion had played a strong part in the development of capitalism and industrialization in Europe.

Noting, as others had done, that the Industrial Revolution took hold earlier and more vigorously in northern Europe, Weber suggested that the Protestant Reformation had been an influential factor. His famous essay *The Protestant Ethic and the Spirit of Capitalism* (1904), published posthumously in book form, took the view that features of Protestantism, and Calvinism in particular, linked it with economic success. Catholics were told of their possible salvation through the authority of a priestly hierarchy that most Protestants lacked. Believing they were predestined for salvation, the Calvinists looked to worldly success as evidence of God's favour. Although some religions, including many Eastern ones, give their followers comfort and consolation in lowly or harrowing circumstances, the Protestant Christian orders sought prosperity as a measure of their acceptability to God, and took success as evidence of it.

Weber pointed to Protestantism's distaste for waste and profligacy (and even generosity), and suggested that this encouraged investment. Combined with Protestant self-discipline and application, this promoted the rational pursuit of wealth. Such factors made Western societies more goal-oriented than their Eastern counterparts, and helped explain their comparative economic success.

In his *Economy and Society* (1921), also published posthumously in book form, Weber embarked on the first modern analysis of the nature of bureaucracy, a work still relevant in modern management studies. He said bureaucracy must have functions bound by explicit rules, feature specialization, and have a hierarchy with a career structure. It must involve salaried jobs, he said, rather than jobs owned by the bureaucrats, and must be dispassionate in its execution rather than politically or personally partisan.

His concern with systems led him to study the impact upon them of factors such as ethnicity and nationalism, as well as religion, and he pioneered the definition of the state through its monopoly on the legitimate use of force.

Although trained in law, Weber spent his life in teaching and scholarship. He sided with Germany in World War I, helping as a director of army hospitals, but his own health was never robust, and he was a victim of the Spanish flu pandemic.

78. Bertrand Russell
1872–1970

Bertrand Russell founded the analytic school of philosophy, thus becoming one of the twentieth century's most influential thinkers. He also earned acclaim as someone who could explain complex topics in clear language accessible to non-professional readers, winning him a Nobel prize in literature. His political activism made him a household name as a pacifist and anti-nuclear campaigner.

He was a grandson of Earl Russell, one of Queen Victoria's prime ministers, and later inherited the title himself. After a degree and then a fellowship at Trinity College, Cambridge, he abandoned the idealist philosophy which he had favoured, and with it the search for all-embracing 'systems', turning his attention instead to logical analysis. His *Principles of Mathematics* (1903) argued that mathematics was a subset of logic, with its truths deduced from logical axioms and thus certain and objective.

In Russell's *On Denoting* (1905), he reworked descriptions of non-real things like 'the present king of France'. Some had claimed that to name something gave it some kind of existence, but Russell argued that such descriptions did not function as names.

What Russell called the 'intellectual high point' of his life came with *Principia Mathematica* (1910–13), which he co-authored with Whitehead. Its logical derivation of mathematics was acclaimed, while its philosophical analysis exposed how conventional language and grammar often diverge from the true logical forms. It set philosophers down the analytical path which led to the linguistic school and logical positivism, and away from grandiose metaphysical systems.

'Russell's Paradox' concerned self-containing sets. The statement 'My father, the village barber, shaves all those and only those who do not shave themselves' has a problem, in that if he does not shave himself, he is shaved by the village barber (himself), and vice versa. Russell modified set theory, proposing a hierarchy of types of set to escape the paradox.

Russell paid for his pacifist agitation with imprisonment during World War I and the loss of his Trinity fellowship. He later became president of the Campaign for Nuclear Disarmament, and was imprisoned a second time after a demonstration.

His talent for popular writing was established in works like *ABC of Atoms* (1923) and *ABC of Relativity* (1925), while his *History of Western Philosophy* (1945) was the century's greatest selling philosophy book, and remains a best-seller. His 1927 lecture 'Why I am not a Christian' brought controversy, especially in the US. He sometimes called himself 'agnostic' because he could not disprove God, helpfully adding that he could not disprove the Homeric gods either.

79. G. E. Moore
1873–1958

G. E. Moore was (with Russell and Wittgenstein) one of the Cambridge philosophers who broke English philosophy from the idealism of Hegel and Kant, and set it on a distinctive, analytical course. Moore switched to philosophy at Cambridge, winning a fellowship, and returning after a brief absence to spend his life there. He was involved with the Bloomsbury Group, which included Strachey, Woolf and Keynes, and belonged to the Apostles, the secret debating society discredited years afterwards by its KGB spies.

Moore was concerned that philosophy had not made the advances which science had seen, and brought to it an exactness and a concern with language that made him a founder of the analytical school. He opposed the fundamentals of idealism in *The Refutation of Idealism* (1903), *In Defence of Common Sense* (1925) and *Proof of an External World* (1939). He says that those claiming the nature of the world is mental, consisting of perceptions, are making assumptions less convincing than the common-sense view that a real world of physical objects exists. He concludes from the statements 'Here is one hand' and 'Here is another' the existence of two objects in a world external to the mind, and says the task of philosophy is not to question the truth of these common-sense beliefs, but to draw out their significance.

Moore's great work, *Principia Ethica* (1903), deals with the 'Naturalistic Fallacy'. You cannot define 'good' in terms of other qualities like happiness, he says, because the question 'Is happiness always good?' is an open one, not trivial or self-evident. Philosophers can discover other properties attached to the good, but they do not define it by doing so. These are 'other' properties, not the same thing. Good cannot be defined; we can only point to good things which illustrate it.

Because Moore says that 'good' cannot be explained, only intuited, some called him an ethical intuitionist. He denied this, claiming that while the nature of good itself is intuitive, the questions we ask about the duties arising from it, which constitute ethical behaviour, are not. Moore thought actions had to be judged by their consequences, empirically ascertained.

The statement, 'It will rain, but I don't believe that it will' was called 'Moore's Paradox', in that it seems absurd that anyone should assert both parts simultaneously, yet there is no logical contradiction involved. It raises questions about what is involved in assertion and belief, and influenced Wittgenstein's own studies into philosophy and language.

80. Pierre Teilhard de Chardin
1881–1955

Pierre Teilhard de Chardin combined the career of a Jesuit priest with that of a paleontologist and a geologist. In youth he had wept when his beloved plough rusted, and resolved to seek eternal and incorruptible things. He studied science, especially paleontology, and participated in important digs, including Piltdown, site of the famous scientific hoax. He later became a Catholic priest and a Jesuit.

In World War I he received the Légion d'honneur for bravery as a stretcher-bearer, and afterwards studied science at the Sorbonne. Friction with his Jesuit authorities began in 1925 when he was ordered to stop teaching, recant his views on original sin, and embark on a geological expedition to China. Teilhard's scientific work showed him the evidence for evolution in rocks and fossils, whereas his order favoured the biblical account of creation. These disputes dogged his life, leading to a posthumous papal reprimand declaring his works to 'offend Catholic doctrine', and moves to 'protect the minds, particularly of the youth' from his works.

During a series of important expeditions to China he published *The Divine Milieu* (1927), which described a personal god at the centre of an *evolving* creation. This conflicted with the teaching that creation was completed 6,000 years ago. But Teilhard did not take Genesis literally. 'Evolution is a light illuminating all fact,' he said, 'a curve that all lines must follow.' In his *Phenomenon of Man* (1938), he tried to reconcile his religious beliefs with scientific discoveries, but the Church forbade its publication and it only appeared after his death.

Teilhard saw the universe as having a direction and purpose toward the evolution of consciousness. He proposed that matter has a tendency to arrange itself in ever more complex arrangements. Particles arranged themselves into inert matter, then

plants, animals and finally man. With mankind came self-consciousness. Teilhard proposed a 'Law of complexity and consciousness' which saw complexity ascending into self-awareness.
With human consciousness came what Teilhard called the
'noosphere', the realm of reflective thought. Crucially, thought
developed from matter; they were aspects of the same thing.

The universe moves towards greater consciousness because it
is pulled along by 'a higher pole of supreme consciousness'
which Teilhard called 'The Omega Point', declaring it to be a
transcendental personal being unlimited by space and time. This
reconciliation of science and God satisfied Teilhard, but not the
Church, while critics have pointed out that in a star-packed
universe Teilhard limited his attention to a single planet.

81. Erwin Schrödinger
1887–1961

Erwin Schrödinger had a major impact on the way we think about reality and the universe we inhabit. He worked in the exciting infancy of quantum and nuclear physics, but found the political world rather too exciting, first leaving Germany when Hitler came to power, and then Austria after Germany absorbed it.

Scientists already knew that subatomic particles were wave-like in some aspects of behaviour. Schrödinger was the first to derive the wave equation, now called 'Schrödinger's wave equation'. He analyzed electrons not as if they were orbiting the nucleus like satellites going around a planet but in terms of wave functions rather than particles, with a 'sphere of probability' for the electron.

This discovery gained him the 1933 Nobel Prize in Physics, but two other ventures also won him acclaim. In 1944 he published *What is Life?*, describing life as an island of negative entropy, temporarily reversing the natural tendency of the universe to run downhill. Because of its organization, life can take in energy to sustain its complexity. He suggested that the molecular structure of the gene could contain the miniature code for life's development. This inspired both Crick and Watson to research the structure of the DNA molecule.

And in 1935 Schrödinger devised a 'thought experiment' in response to the Copenhagen interpretation of quantum mechanics. At the subatomic level the position and velocity of an electron could not both be measured simultaneously. The determination of their value occurred with the act of measurement. This might work for the subatomic universe, but Schrödinger ingeniously links this world with the everyday world.

He asks us to consider a cat locked inside a box with a radioactive particle which might or might not decay within the hour. If it does, a relay will trigger the release of cyanide and poison the cat. Schrödinger asks if, after an hour, the cat is alive or dead? Since the decay has not been measured, it has not yet fulfilled either of its possibilities. Only when the box is opened will that occur. In effect, the cat is neither alive nor dead (or both) until the box is opened. This is a genuine paradox, one reason why scientists, including Einstein, have been troubled by the implications of quantum mechanics.

Schrödinger's private life, with wife and mistress sharing his household, was too exotic for a position at either Oxford or Yale. It did not, however, prevent a splendid crater on the moon's dark side being named after him.

82. Martin Heidegger
   1889–1976

Martin Heidegger was hailed as a leading existentialist philosopher (captivating Sartre among others), though he emphatically rejected the title. His thinking has certainly influenced continental philosophy, though his obscure, at times impenetrable, language made him less significant in the Anglo-American analytic tradition. His reputation was clouded by his links with the Nazi party and his statements in support of it.

He had a religious childhood, enrolling as a Jesuit novice, then studying theology at Freiburg, where he later taught philosophy under the influence of Husserl. Husserl appointed him his successor, though Heidegger's views had diverged from his mentor's.

In *Being and Time* (1927) and *What is Metaphysics?* (1929) he asked the question, 'What is nothing?' Logic says the negative comes from something positive, but Heidegger wants us to examine just Nothing itself, so he moves beyond logic. When we think about Nothing, we are aware of our moods, in particular the feeling of dread it arouses in us – the 'angst' of existentialism.

We exist, he says, yet 'being-there' involves the awareness of our ultimate death, a fact that is ever present in our lives. Death is thus a factor in life; it shapes it. In a similar way, Heidegger tells us, 'Nothing' shapes Being. It is not the opposite of Being, but its concomitant.

In asking 'What does it mean for someone to be?' Heidegger looked at 'ways of being', and tried to examine them not by empirical philosophy but by phenomenology, the self-evident insight into the structure of experience. He thought that contemporary 'ways of being' were inauthentic, in that humans had lost the truths of their primitive world, and were absorbed in a one-sided technological culture, alienating them.

Heidegger felt the appeal of communion with nature, and for

a time tried the simple, peasant life. He thought that although people lived in a world they had been 'thrown into' and could be absorbed by, they were free to choose and to direct themselves. Only at death did these possibilities cease. He said, 'Every man is born as many men and dies as a single one.'

Heidegger touched a rising wave of German romanticism which hailed the aesthetic, poetic and mythological power of philosophy, and found one outlet in Nazism. When Hitler became chancellor in 1933, Heidegger became rector of Freiburg University and spoke on 'The Role of the University in the New Reich'. After World War II Heidegger was banned from teaching for five years as punishment for not opposing Nazi ideas.

83. Ludwig Wittgenstein
   1889–1951

'The world is everything that is the case' is the famous line of twentieth-century philosophy which opens Ludwig Wittgenstein's *Tractatus Logico-Philosophicus* (1922).

Wittgenstein was the youngest of eight children of a very wealthy Austrian family, all musical and talented, but prone to depression. Three of his four brothers killed themselves, and Wittgenstein himself experienced depressive phases, sometimes needing to retreat to isolated dwellings. Starting in mechanical engineering, Wittgenstein was drawn to Russell at Cambridge, joining the English analytic school of philosophy.

His thought is often divided between the 'earlier' Wittgenstein of the *Tractatus* and the 'later' Wittgenstein of his posthumous *Philosophical Investigations* (1953). The *Tractatus* establishes a close relationship between language, mind, and reality. The world consists of independent 'atomic' facts, or states of affairs, out of which larger facts can be built. Language consists of 'atomic' propositions out of which larger ones can be built, and thought and language 'picture' the states of affairs they refer to. Wittgenstein uses the analogy that words create a picture of what they represent, a picture containing elements corresponding to what it represents and mirroring the logical structure of the state of affairs it pictures. Meaning thus involves a direct reference to the real, and if the elements of a proposition have no such reference, no sense can be conveyed.

The Vienna Circle of logical positivists took Wittgenstein's 'atomic' propositions to be elements of experience, and therefore dismissed as nonsense all statements which referred neither to tautological truths nor to ones validated by experience. This took out most of philosophy's traditional concerns, including ethics, religion and aesthetics. Wittgenstein himself was less dogmatic, pointing to things which, although unsayable, can be shown.

He was even less dogmatic in his *Investigations*, now treating language as part of life, used differently in different contexts, and shifting meanings over time. He called the different uses 'language games', examining the rules that apply within particular games. He wanted to free philosophy from the 'bewitchments' that came from misuse of language. Language, he said, is part of life; when it enters metaphysics it lacks reference points. He compared it to sliding around on frictionless ice without the 'rough ground' of everyday life to steady it.

Wittgenstein admitted that his *Tractatus* broke its own rules of sense, adding that after climbing it, one had to kick away the ladder that led there. But his view remained that the philosopher's task was to reduce confusions of language, thereby dissolving, rather than solving, many philosophical problems.

84. Herbert Marcuse
1898–1979

Herbert Marcuse was one of the most popular and widely read philosophers of his day, reaching the height of his celebrity in the 1960s, and dubbed the 'Father of the New Left'. His fame did not endure, perhaps because his audience was at a popular, not an academic, level.

His philosophy remained within the Hegelian and Marxist traditions throughout his life. He had participated in the unsuccessful left-wing Spartacist uprising in Germany in 1919, and as the Nazis rose to power he fled to Switzerland and then to the USA, where he made his home.

Marcuse applied Hegelian and Marxist ideas to modern social theory in *Reason and Revolution* (1941), but it was two of his later works which brought him fame. He published *Eros and Civilization* in 1955, and *One Dimensional Man* in 1964. The former attempted a synthesis of the ideas of Marx and Freud, seeking the path to a more liberated society at just the time when the post-war generation was seeking to loosen the old restrictions and taboos. Looking at Freud's assertion that civilization of necessity involves repression, Marcuse argues that Freud in fact reveals evidence of an unconscious human drive towards freedom and happiness, one which shows in cultural activities. Marcuse sketches out what a non-repressive society might be like, without alienation of labour, and with free space for play and a liberated sexuality. It was a vision attractive to student radicals seeking greater freedom.

Marcuse's *One Dimensional Man* achieved cult status as a critique of the repressive nature of capitalist, industrial societies. His thesis is that the old oppressors have been replaced by more subtle social controls. The revolutionary potential of the working classes has been subverted by the 'false needs' generated by modern society, sucking people into a web of production and consumption. 'The people recognize themselves in their commodities; they find their soul in their automobile, hi-fi set, split-level home, kitchen equipment,' he says, and the mass media and advertising all contribute to this, creating a one-dimensional society which compromises the ability to think outside and beyond it. Society subordinates people to its productive mechanisms.

This found ready ears in a generation disaffected by both capitalism and communism, but Marcuse trod on more controversial ground with his essay *Repressive Tolerance* (1965), arguing that modern tolerance is repressive by permitting repressive speech a voice, and allowing 'inauthentic' ideas to be propagated. Some critics saw this as a justification to ban disagreement with New Left ideas.

85. Friedrich Hayek
1899–1992

Friedrich von Hayek was one of the twentieth century's greatest and most effective opponents of collectivism and central planning. His doctorates (in law and political science) were gained in the intellectual powerhouse of early 1920s Vienna, after service in the Austro-Hungarian army in World War I. In Vienna he was influenced by the economic thinking of Ludwig von Mises, and it was in economics that he won his Nobel Prize in 1974.

At the LSE in the 1930s, Hayek was among the few opponents of Keynesian economics, and published works setting out the Austrian School case founded on methodological individualism, building up from motivated actions by individual participants, rather than downwards from large-scale macroeconomic equations.

Hayek achieved international fame with his *Road to Serfdom* (1944), written partly to show the socialist roots of Nazism, but also to warn that central planning necessitates compulsion and systematic erosion of liberty. Popular fame came with the 1948 Reader's Digest's condensed version addressed to a mass audience.

When at Chicago, Hayek published *The Constitution of Liberty* (1960) on the centenary of Mill's *On Liberty*, setting out the merits of a free social and economic order, and identifying the errors and adverse consequences of central planning.

Several themes dominate Hayek's thinking. One is the 'knowledge problem', that those who would plan society cannot access the required knowledge. It is dispersed and often ephemeral. Knowledge is contained within society, though, and people act on signals such as the price mechanism, which Hayek identified as a transmitter of information.

Society's order is spontaneous, says Hayek, 'the result of human action, but not of human design'. It responds to the actions of its participants, containing more knowledge than a planned system, and is speedier to react to events. It has evolved over time and been tested by circumstance. Hayek's *The Fatal Conceit* (1988) deals with the delusion that individual minds can think up societies superior to those created spontaneously by millions.

In *The Counter-Revolution of Science* (1955), Hayek identifies the limits of knowledge about social studies, describing 'scientism' as the view that the methods of the physical sciences can be applied to them. He deals with complex orders in which simple linear predictions do not work, undermining those seeking to remake societies in conformity with preconceived ideas.

Hayek instigated the post-war Mont Pelerin Society, which argued for free societies and free economies, and lived to see his life's work vindicated by the collapse of the socialist economies and their totalitarian societies.

86. Gilbert Ryle
     1900–1976

Gilbert Ryle, who taught philosophy at Oxford and served in intelligence in World War II, belonged to the English analytical school, and was influenced by Russell and Wittgenstein.

He regarded philosophy's task to be 'the detection of the sources in linguistic idioms of recurrent misconceptions and absurd theories', publishing *Systematically Misleading Expressions* (1932) to show how language can lead to logical error. He identifies 'category mistakes' in which two things are placed in logically equivalent categories because of a grammatical equivalence. The sentence 'She came home in a sedan chair and a flood of tears' should not lead us to suppose that a flood of tears constitute a form of personal transportation like a sedan chair.

Ryle's most famous book, *The Concept of Mind* (1949), was said 'to have put the last nail in the coffin of Cartesian dualism'. In it he rejects Descartes' separation of mind and body into separate categories as an idea from before our understanding of biology. It is confusing, says Ryle, to consider a human body which exists in space and is subject to mechanical laws, and then add a mysterious entity which is neither. His memorable phrase describes it as like a 'ghost in the machine'. The mind is in fact 'a set of capacities and abilities belonging to the body', and is merely the body's intelligent behaviour, he suggests.

He denies that a thought must precede every action, pointing out that a thought is itself an action. Is it preceded by the thought of a thought? he asks, identifying the infinite series known as 'Ryle's Regress'.

Ryle controversially claims that every mental activity must refer to witnessable (rather than private) activities, or behaviour, and that behaviour 'need never refer to anything but the operations of human bodies'. Mental statements can be translated into ones about what individuals will (or might) do under certain circumstances. Some called this philosophical behaviourism, reformulating mental talk in terms of behaviour rather than an inner life. Ryle allowed for the 'internal mono- logue or silent soliloquy' of an inner life, making him only a 'weak' behaviourist.

Ryle compared philosophy to map-making. We speak lan- guage as we have absorbed it, much like a villager knows his way around his village by habit. But in philosophy we have to know that expressions have 'implication threads' which sometimes conflict. He uses the example of a weary sailor in a storm 'having toiled voluntarily, although reluctantly', observing that the two adverbs seem to conflict unless one knows the general notions governing their use.

Ryle's own language was commendably clear; indeed, he was part of philosophy's 'ordinary language' movement.

87. Michael Oakeshott
1901–1990

Michael Oakeshott was a major philosopher of conservatism, though he chose an academic rather than a political career. The traditionalist strand of conservative philosophy, which treats it in Lord Cecil's words as 'a disposition averse from change', was lucky to have had two immensely powerful and eloquent writers: Burke and Oakeshott.

Oakeshott highlights two elements of conservatism: there is the affection and comfort which accompanies familiar things; and there is a profound scepticism of man's ability to improve his society or his circumstances through rational analysis. Indeed, it is rationalism that Oakeshott attacks in his essay *Rationalism in Politics* (1962). He is not opposed to rational thought, just to the inappropriate use of it in areas which call for other types of experience. Politics, he says, is an area in which rational thought has been overused.

Rationalists have tried to analyze society, Oakeshott says, but in doing so they necessarily reduce it and miss important elements. Moral ideas are like a sediment suspended in a religious or social tradition, he says, and cannot simply be filtered out and examined in isolation.

The art of politics is not about seeking to perfect society, and there is no ultimate goal. In a famous metaphor he says that 'In political activity, then, men sail a boundless and bottomless sea; there is neither harbour for shelter nor floor for anchorage, neither starting place nor appointed destination.' The object is to keep afloat, and to use 'the resources of a traditional manner of behaviour in order to make a friend of every hostile occasion'.

Those who try to achieve a perfect society by applying rational and scientific principles run the risk of losing what is of value, and what has stood the test of time. The wise man, says Oakeshott, contents himself with the opportunities for fulfilment and satisfaction in what is already available. The conservative disposition lacks the restless utopianism which preoccupies radical thinkers, but seeks satisfaction in the here and now instead.

In his essay *On Being Conservative*, Oakeshott sets out the characteristics which make up that disposition. 'To be conservative,' he writes, 'is to prefer the familiar to the unknown, to prefer the tried to the untried, fact to mystery, the actual to the possible, the limited to the unbounded, the near to the distant, the sufficient to the superabundant, the convenient to the perfect, present laughter to utopian bliss.' It is a powerful and eloquent attack on man's constant quest for improvement and perfection.

88. Karl Popper
   1902–1994

Alfred Adler, famed for identifying the inferiority complex, was referred by the teenaged Karl Popper to a new case 'which did not seem particularly Adlerian'. Adler immediately explained it in terms of inferiority complexes. 'I know it,' he told the young Popper, 'from my thousand-fold experience.' Popper replied that he supposed it was now a thousand and one, with none of the other 'examples' being any more impressive. Popper recognized that a theory which purports to explain everything tells us nothing, and that only theories which could be refuted can extend knowledge.

Of the theories then in vogue, Popper realized that no circumstance could refute those of Freud, Adler or Marx, whereas Einstein's could be shown to be wrong if observation went against it. Popper published *Logik der Forschung* (1934), setting out his analysis of scientific method. In English it became *The Logic of Scientific Discovery* (1959).

Popper overturned the idea that science proceeds by induction, producing theories from repeated observations, and then proving them by experiment. Instead, Popper says that it needs a theory to highlight observations, to give them significance, and that we conjecture theories to solve problems. Experiments can never prove theories, says Popper, but they can refute them. There is an asymmetry between verification and falsification because no number of test passes can ever prove a theory finally true, whereas just one counter-example can undermine it. The valuable theories are those which could be proved wrong but are not, because these are the ones that enable us to predict and test unlikely circumstances.

Unlike the logical positivists, Popper does not dismiss metaphysics as nonsense. He does separate statements, however, into science and non-science. Scientific statements are those which can be tested and possibly refuted. Popper thus sees science as a body of provisional knowledge which proceeds by eliminating theories that have been falsified. He describes this as 'objective knowledge', claiming that it corresponds to the truth.

Popper's scientific philosophy illuminates his social and political outlook. He was forced to flee Austria when it was absorbed by Nazi Germany, and spent the war writing in New Zealand. In *The Poverty of Historicism* (1944), he attacks the claim that history is leading to an inevitable conclusion as just another untestable, unscientific assertion used to justify fanaticism and oppression. He continues in *The Open Society and its Enemies* (1945) with a passionate attack on Plato, Hegel and Marx as totalitarian apologists, and with a spirited defence of open, democratic societies which engage in 'piecemeal social engineering', instead of attempting to impose a preconceived new order.

89. Arthur Koestler
1905–1983

Arthur Koestler symbolized the philosophical movement of many European intellectuals during the twentieth century in response to its turbulent events. Of Jewish Hungarian background, he was swept along and shaped by some of those events. He never completed the psychology degree he studied in 1920s Vienna, but worked in a kibbutz in Palestine, and then did propaganda for the Comintern, having joined the Communist Party in 1931.

The 1938 Stalin show trials in Moscow profoundly affected his outlook, and he left the Communist Party to become one of its most effective critics. His experiences informed his most famous novel, *Darkness at Noon* (1940), but it was also illuminated by his own experiences of prison. A UK newspaper correspondent in the Spanish Civil War, he was captured and sentenced to death by Franco's forces. He spent several months in prison, hearing men executed each day before he was released in an exchange.

Darkness at Noon is a political fictionalization of Stalin's show trials, in which the protagonist, Rubashov, first denies and then confesses to crimes he did not commit. Koestler answers the question 'why?' by suggesting that violent revolutions corrupt those who stage them. Rubashov confesses because 'justice and objective truth have long ceased to have any meaning for him' (as Orwell puts it); his soul has been corrupted by the Communist Party. In *The God that Failed* (1950), Koestler assembles a group of former communist intellectuals to set out why they became disillusioned and abandoned their dream.

Throughout his life Koestler was interested in the paranormal, and even endowed a posthumous chair in it at Edinburgh University. He experienced LSD with Tim Leary, but disagreed with Aldous Huxley's view that its hallucinations gave meaningful insights. On the contrary, he said, 'they are in the nature of confidence tricks played on one's own nervous system'.

In *The Ghost in the Machine* (1960), Koestler deals with the tensions between man's more primitive emotional responses and the rational activity which emerged later. Koestler is convinced that humanity's instinctive responses would lead it to self-annihilation, and suggests chemical modification of the brain to prevent this.

He travelled in India and Japan, examining Eastern meditative and transcendental systems such as yoga and zen to see if they could improve the nature of Western thought, but wrote *The Lotus and the Robot* to describe his failure – 'I started my journey in sackcloth and ashes, and came back rather proud of being a European.'

90. Ayn Rand
1905–1982

Ayn Rand's philosophy was largely expressed in her fiction writing. An exile from post-revolutionary Russia, she settled in the US and began script writing in Hollywood. Her works included *For the New Intellectual* (1961), *Capitalism – the Unknown Ideal* (1966) and *An Introduction to Objectivist Epistemology* (1979), but it is her popular novels which disseminated her ideas most widely.

Her first best-seller, *The Fountainhead* (1943), features a brilliant architect who refuses to compromise his principles. He embodies a radical individualism central to Rand's philosophy. The book's success, and that of its movie adaptation starring Gary Cooper, projected Rand to a wider audience. Her later work, *Atlas Shrugged* (1957), depicting a mysterious strike by leading innovators and industrialists, still sells hundreds of thousands of copies a year.

Rand called her philosophy 'objectivism', deriving it, like Aristotle and Aquinas, from so-called axioms, or self-evident principles. The primary is that reality exists as an objective absolute, independently of any conscious mind. Anything that exists has a specific nature. A thing is what it is; its characteristics constitute its identity. Consciousness is the faculty of perceiving things that exist.

Essential to Rand's system is the idea that knowledge is gained volitionally, by the active use of reason, not automatically by faith or revelation.

Rand held that human life is the standard of moral value, and that reason is a human being's basic means of survival. She concluded that individuals should be the beneficiaries of their own actions. People have the right to pursue their rational self-interest (including life, liberty and owning property). This is not to be equated with instant, transitory, gratification. Rather, it is the systematic enhancement of one's life. In Rand's view there is no conflict of interests between rational individuals; they recognize the value of respecting each other's rights consistently, sacrificing neither themselves nor others. All can gain from the creativity of free individuals. The initiation of physical force is anathema to the reasoning mind.

She said, 'My philosophy, in essence, is the concept of man as a heroic being, with his own happiness as the moral purpose of his life, with productive achievement as his noblest activity, and reason as his only absolute.' This led her to espouse laissez-faire capitalism, and to oppose any government action beyond those needed to protect individual rights.

Rand has a huge following today, especially among young people, attracted by her philosophy of rational individualism, and by the way the objectivism of knowledge meshes in with its ethical and political stance.

91. Jean-Paul Sartre
1905–1980

Jean-Paul Sartre was the most famous French philosopher of the twentieth century, but always had a larger following among the public intelligentsia than in the halls of academe. This might be because he chose to play to a public audience. The enduring image of Sartre has him where he liked to be, in a café, cigarette in one hand, coffee in the other, and with an admiring audience hanging on his words.

Sartre was the voice of the post-war generation, and was partly shaped by his education in the elitist Ecole Normal Supérieure. Conscripted as a meteorologist in France's army, he was captured and imprisoned by the Germans in 1940, but released on health grounds after a year. The loss of freedom in captivity probably confirmed the views about freedom which he expressed in plays, novels, political writing and philosophical papers.

At the heart of his philosophy was existentialism. This separates 'being-*in*-itself' from 'being-*for*-itself'. Basically, there are things that exist in themselves, things like solid objects which do not change until they are destroyed. Then there are humans, conscious beings who exist *for* themselves. The point is that human beings are not defined or fixed like the other objects. They make themselves by their decisions and their actions. A human is not completely defined until they are dead, and no longer able to change themselves.

In *Being and Nothingness* (1943), Sartre makes the point that man is alone, without support, and fully responsible for what he is. Man creates his own 'essence' by the way he lives, and thus, uniquely for mankind, his existence precedes his essence. He is free, 'terrifyingly free', said Sartre, to experience the anguish of total responsibility for himself.

Sartre emphasized life's lack of any outside purpose.

'Everything that exists is born for no reason, carries on living through weakness, and dies by accident,' he wrote. Man's total freedom is oppressive because of that burden of responsibility; he is 'condemned to be free'. Sartre's play *Huis Clos* (1944) is set in hell, where the characters no longer have the freedom to change themselves, but can only torment each other eternally – hence the play's message, 'hell is other people'.

Sartre thought writers had a duty to participate in social and political issues, and was an apologist first for Soviet communism, then for radical New Left ideas, describing Ché Guevara as 'the era's most perfect man'. On political grounds he publicly declined the Nobel Prize awarded him in 1964.

92. Hannah Arendt
1906–1976

Hannah Arendt contributed significantly to twentieth-century political philosophy, choosing the themes of power and freedom. Born into a middle-class German Jewish family of Russian origins, she experienced first hand some of the tumultuous events that shaped the century. She studied philosophy with Husserl and Heidegger (having an affair with the latter), but was arrested by the Gestapo and fled to France. Escaping internment there in World War II, she made her subsequent career in the US.

The Origins of Totalitarianism (1951) brought her acclaim and controversy, for she treated Stalin's communism and Hitler's Nazism as alike, originating from the collapse of traditional political orders. Totalitarianism was a new form of government, she said, made possible by the collapse of the territorial nation states under the impact of imperialism, and by the tendency of people to identify with a race instead of a citizenry or a class. The turmoil of World War I and the Great Depression led people to seek a clear path to the future, offered by totalitarian regimes with their supposed laws of history. Terror and ideology were now used to control, justified by those selfsame 'laws'.

In *The Human Condition* (1958), she looked at labour, work and action, and what they had enabled in previous cultures that was now lost. Her thesis was that Western philosophy had lost its concern with action and the world of experience, and retreated, starting with Plato, into a concern with the abstract and the essences behind things. People had thereby lost their ability to renew by creative activity, seeking divine solutions instead of ones gained through worldly activity.

In *On Revolution* (1963), Arendt opposed the notion that historical forces shaped revolutions, insisting that their essence lay in human actions. The successful revolution for her was the American Revolution, whereas the French and Russian ones failed to achieve their objectives. She approved of Jefferson's idea for small townships, and the public participatory freedom they embodied.

Controversy returned with her coverage of the Eichmann trial in Israel (for Holocaust crimes), and her book *Eichmann in Jerusalem* (1963). She treated Eichmann as more bureaucrat than monster, and coined the phrase 'the banality of evil'. Eichmann was 'terrifyingly normal', she declared, and 'this normality was more terrifying that all of the atrocities put together'. It showed what ordinary people could come to.

Arendt was honored in her day, becoming Princeton's first female full professor, and has been honoured since by having an asteroid named after her.

H. L. A. Hart was among the twentieth century's most significant legal philosophers. As professor of jurisprudence at Oxford, he brought analytical philosophy into the study of law. He was an exponent of positive, as opposed to natural, law, and maintained that the law should not be used to enforce society's morality.

Hart was concerned to reject Austin's view, that law is the expression of the sovereign's will backed by coercion. Hart took the view that laws are made by humans to serve their purposes, and that there is no necessary connection between law and morality. This contrasts with natural law, which takes laws to derive from a universal human nature and be valid everywhere.

In *The Concept of Law* (1961), Hart asserted that law and coercion are no more necessarily linked than are law and morality. The existence of legal rights, he said, might be in the absence of any moral justification. Our duty to obey the law stems from the general rules of our society, not from the coercion imposed by authority.

Hart debated the point in books and lectures against Lord Devlin, who maintained that laws should impose morality to prevent the destruction of society. In his *Law, Liberty and Morality* (1963), Hart followed Mill's tradition by saying that the law should limit its activity to stopping people harming each other. An activity that has no victims should not be a crime.

There is no evidence, says Hart, that society is defined by its morality, or that immorality threatens it. On the contrary, morality changes over time without its society being destroyed. And the benefits of democracy do not justify a majority imposing its will on a dissenting minority, or threatening their life, liberty or property.

Hart distinguished between immorality that might affront public decency, and that which merely distressed people that it was happening in private. Law might outlaw public expressions of bigamy or prostitution, but not purely private expression of them.

The debate's importance surfaced in the 1957 Wolfenden Report which recommended that homosexuality and prostitution performed in private should not be illegal. All the Wolfenden Committee's members save Lord Devlin took the Hart view, saying 'There must remain a realm of private morality and immorality which is, in brief and crude terms, none of the law's business,' whereas Devlin said, 'The suppression of vice is as much the law's business as the suppression of subversive activities.' Hart's views ultimately prevailed, and the report's recommendations were implemented.

94. Isaiah Berlin
1909–1997

Isaiah Berlin, one of the most celebrated scholars of his day, said he would leave no disciples because he had no body of doctrine to define his thought. That was the point; he was the leading advocate of pluralism and toleration, arguing that there are no single ideas that encapsulate human ideas or history.

Born a Russian Jew in Riga (in present-day Latvia), in boyhood he had seen communist police seize and remove a man, and formed a lifelong aversion to tyranny. His family left for Britain in 1920 when he was 11, and he made it his home, winning a fellowship at All Souls and making his career in Oxford.

Berlin is noted for his *Two Concepts of Liberty* (1958), distinguishing between negative and positive liberty. Negative liberty, urged by Mill, allows people freedom to act without interference by others. Positive liberty allows people to mould their own destiny and to achieve self-mastery and self-realization.

The two can conflict, leading to a trade-off between people's desire to make their own decisions and a desire to help people control their circumstances. Berlin expresses concern that the idea of positive freedom is prone to abuse by political ideologies, having seen totalitarian regimes enslave millions in its name. He is a firm pluralist, believing there is no single truth or principle, but that life is made up of compromises between competing values, often incompatible. Freedom and equality might both be noble, but they often conflict. He develops these themes in *Four Essays on Liberty* (1969).

In *The Hedgehog and the Fox* (1953), Berlin brings similar reasoning to the study of history. The book explores Tolstoy's approach, observing that 'the fox knows many things, but the hedgehog knows one big thing' (Archilochus). Berlin again takes the pluralist view: there is no single organizing principle behind history, as Hegel and Marx suppose. He is sceptical of the view that exceptional individuals direct history, as he is of historical determinism by great forces. There are no laws of history corresponding to scientific laws, and while scientific method is useful, the historian has to deploy concepts which interpret and explain.

In our moral lives, too, Berlin denies any single moral axiom such as utilitarianism. There are competing, human-made values, with no fixed standard to dictate choice, but always conflicts and compromises.

An amusing anecdote tells how Prime Minister Winston Churchill, saying he'd 'better meet this fellow, Berlin', bemusedly found himself having lunch with the American songwriter Irving Berlin.

95. A. J. Ayer
1910–1989

A. J. Ayer was among Britain's most influential twentieth-century philosophers, more for the clarity and directness with which he expounded ideas than for any major innovative contributions. Educated on scholarships at Eton and Oxford, and from a Dutch Jewish background, Ayer served in Special Operations in World War II, and was celebrated thereafter as a charismatic lecturer and broadcaster.

Fame came early. He had attended meetings of the Vienna Circle of logical positivists, influenced in particular by Schlick, and set out an English version of their approach in *Language, Truth and Logic*, completed before his 25th birthday and published in 1936.

Ayer draws on the empirical tradition of David Hume and the logical positivism of Vienna. There are two different types of knowledge, he says. There is empirical knowledge gained through sensory impressions, and there is analytic knowledge, true by definition, which expresses our determination to use language in certain ways. Ayer goes much further, though, saying that propositions are devoid of any meaning at all unless they are analytic, or capable, at least in principle, of being empirically verified.

Ayer thus declares metaphysical speculation to be meaningless, since it is not susceptible to empirical test, and he scorns the continental tradition of philosophical speculation, as well as the work of many of his British contemporaries: it did not make him popular with either. Ayer himself modified his expression in response to criticism, but was never able to rebut the claim that *nothing* could be empirically proven without the possibility of some new fact overturning it. Popper categorized untestable statements not as nonsense, as Ayer did, but as non-science, and then only if they could never be proved *false*.

Ayer developed his ideas in *The Problem of Knowledge* (1956) and in his 1972–3 Gifford lectures, published as *The Central Questions of Philosophy*. He remained committed to the view that many of the apparent problems which had preoccupied philosophers came down to problems of language, rather than providing any real insights into reality and its experience.

Although his combative style provoked opposition, Ayer did highlight one problem of metaphysical speculation – the difficulty in comparing and evaluating propositions which are not susceptible to any testing process. Ayer became Wykeham Professor at Oxford and was knighted for services to philosophy. He also led a full social life which included four marriages, and expressed the wish that he could have been a tap dancer. He once confronted boxer Mike Tyson, protecting model Naomi Campbell from Tyson's unwanted advances by suggesting they should 'talk about this like rational men'.

96. John Rawls
1921–2002

During 40 years as a Harvard philosophy professor, John Rawls reinvigorated political philosophy with strikingly original ideas. His book *A Theory of Justice* (1971) wove together strands of political, legal and moral philosophy. His aim was to establish the basis of a just society, and his approach was labelled 'justice as fairness'.

Rawls begins with a thought experiment, called the 'original position', in which he imagines there is no society, much as Hobbes and Locke imagined it before a social contract. If there were no society, how would people set it up so as to make it acceptable to all? Being reasonable and rational, they would seek to maximize the benefits it brought, and to minimize any disadvantages.

Rawls explicitly rejects the utilitarian notion seeking the greatest amount of good, proposing instead the greatest *average* level of good achievable. He postulates a 'veil of ignorance', in which those drawing up the rules cannot know where any person, including themselves, might end up. Since they will want to maximize their own chances of well-being, they will opt for a society which gives them equal access to rights and opportunities. It resembles the pie game in which, in order to have two children share a pie without complaint, one child divides the pie and the other has first choice. Since the first child does not know which portion will be his, he creates equal ones.

Two principles are needed, says Rawls. The first (the liberty principle) is that people must have equal claim on basic liberties, and the second (the difference principle) is that economic and social inequalities should be such as to bring greatest benefit to the least advantaged. The basic liberties must be worth having, even to people low on the socio-economic scale, in order that society shall be worth living in, whatever one's status might be.

In the second part of his difference principle, Rawls says that people with similar talents and motivations should have similar chances to make the best of them.

Critics have noted that Rawls, unlike Locke and others, does not include property rights in his basic liberties. Furthermore, he postulates only one model of a just society, leaving no opportunities to opt out, to depart for a different society, or to change the rules. Others have suggested that his second principle expresses, rather than establishes, a preconceived egalitarianism which others might not share, and that he acts as though wealth is just *there*, waiting to be shared, instead of having to be made.

Thomas Kuhn was one of the most celebrated writers on scientific discovery of the late twentieth century, but was acclaimed more by sociologists and scientific historians than by philosophers. Others, most notably Karl Popper, had written about how scientific progress is made, and what makes one explanation preferable to another, but Kuhn wrote instead about how scientists actually behaved in practice, rather than about the rationality of science itself. While a professor at Berkeley, in 1962 he published *The Structure of Scientific Revolutions.*

Kuhn said that scientists were quite attached to their theories, and tried to avoid having to replace them by alternative ones. He said that science did not make continual progress, but was characterized by alternate periods of calm and upheaval. During the quiet periods, which he called 'normal science', what actually happened was a series of puzzle-solving events within the prevailing paradigm, in which apparent anomalies were accommodated and the theory subject to small modifications. The paradigm itself was not open to question, and most scientists worked within it. This was where the research was accepted, and the prizes and promotions won.

However, there came times in particular areas of science when the prevailing theory itself was found inadequate, and the search began for a new paradigm. These were periods of upheaval and uncertainty, in which scientists lacked an accepted paradigm to direct their research. An example was the Ptolemaic or geocentric view of the universe. This was the earth-centred paradigm refined by the addition of cycles and epicycles to allow the theory to accommodate aberrant observations, instead of overthrowing it. This was genuine science, said Kuhn, but the modifications eventually made the theory so unwieldy that science was ready for Copernicus to replace the old paradigm by a new sun-centred account of planetary motion.

Kuhn thought there had to be a shared commitment to a paradigm to enable progress to be made, and that anomalous observations tended to be explained away, and in any case depended on the outlook of the observers. His approach was welcomed by many whose ideas did not stand up to the scrutiny of more rigorous views of scientific method, and his disciples went further than Kuhn himself in advocating a non-rational, more sociological and even political basis for scientific progress. But even though scientists might win the acclaim of their peers, few think this is the test by which their theories are regarded as extending scientific knowledge.

98. Michel Foucault
1926–1984

Michel Foucault, not related to the Leon Foucault whose pendulum showed the earth's rotation, was linked with the philosophy of structuralism, though he denied the label. A twentieth-century French thinker of great range and complexity, Foucault graduated in both psychology and philosophy, but drew on many other disciplines including history and criminology to substantiate his analysis.

He was Professor at the Collège de France of 'History of Systems of Thought', his major field of study. He rejects the idea of history revealing objective truths or teaching universal lessons. Instead, he says that the knowledge available to any epoch is determined (and limited) by that epoch's social norms, its languages, its cultural expressions and the philosophies it espouses. In *The Order of Things* (1966), he says that every age's implicit conditions of truth limit its norms. Every epoch has its *episteme*, or order of knowledge, embedded in the tacit experience of its fundamental codes and outlook.

Foucault uses what he calls the 'archaeological method' to examine the interconnected aspects of culture which give each period its unconscious rules and defining characteristics. In doing so he draws on diverse materials overlooked by more conventional historians. In particular he looks at those whom societies exclude, examining societies by their treatment of outsiders such as insane people, prisoners and sexual deviants. He claims that modern 'humane' responses to such outsiders are subtle ways to control and to exclude. In *Madness and Civilization* (1961), Foucault says that reason has excluded, like lepers, areas previously included. 'Madness,' he says, 'is silenced by Reason, losing its power.'

He studies power, not just the power of individuals, groups and classes but that exercised by forms of discourse and institutional practices, and regards all social relationships as being fundamentally about power relationships, morally disturbing ones. He sees science and reason as instruments of power, and says that modern society represses by its pervasive conformity.

Controversially, and provocatively, Foucault describes the idea of 'man' as a nineteenth-century invention, and predicts the imminent disappearance of 'man' (the idea) because history is now seen as brought about by objective and external forces. He rejects the Hegelian and Marxist idea of a unified history, seeing only breaks in any continuous interpretation, together with the workings of chance.

Foucault espoused left-wing causes, briefly joining the Communist Party and opposing France's Algerian war. His analysis replaced Sartre's existentialism as an inspiration to young French intellectuals, and he greatly influenced historical research into types of social experience.

Noam Chomsky revolutionized linguistic analysis, instigating the move in the US from behaviourist to cognitive psychology, and throwing down serious challenges to empiricist philosophy. While he spent most of his professional life at the Massachusetts Institute of Technology, he had a far wider, non-academic audience as an outspoken critic of US foreign policy, militarism and corporate capitalism.

His books *Syntactic Structures* (1957) and *Aspects of the Theory of Syntax* (1965) challenged the then-prevailing view that language is acquired by children as a set of skills gained from training and experience. Chomsky points to the speed with which children pick up language, and identifies a significant gap between the stimuli they receive and the knowledge they attain.

He identifies two levels of linguistic knowledge: the 'surface structures' represented by the words and sounds used; and the 'deep structures', the *universal grammar* which he says is common to all languages. This knowledge is innate, says Chomsky, and represents a biological capacity of the brain. In effect, his claim is that children are hard-wired for language. They learn the parochial features of their own language, but the rest is innate. They hear adults speaking and infer from that a complex set of grammatical rules enabling them to construct totally new sentences. Chomsky suggests that while these rules are finite in number, the new sentences that can be constructed from them are not.

Chomsky's *Cartesian Linguistics* (1966) attacks the empiricist view that knowledge is gained only by experience. Not only do children acquire language too quickly for that, he says, but children learning different languages do so in similar stages, making similar errors and avoiding similar ones. His review of B. F. Skinner's *Verbal Behaviour* (1959) undermines the notion of behavioural psychologists that children learn languages by stimulus and response. Chomsky's claim is that the proficiency and fluency which children develop so rapidly point instead to an innate grammatical structure already present within them, one which underlies all human languages.

The assumption of a priori knowledge has not commanded universal acceptance. Some critics have suggested that the ability to acquire languages with all their complex rules can be accounted for by the brain's general processing abilities, while Ryle urged close attention to the realities of imitation and practice by which children develop linguistic skills. Chomsky's contribution to the 'nature or nurture' debate was a powerful one, although it was probably his political activities which led *Prospect* magazine's readers to proclaim him in 2005 'the world's leading intellectual'.

100. Jacques Derrida
1930–2004

Jacques Derrida is among the most important of modern French thinkers, and certainly among the most controversial. Attacks by leading intellectuals have charged him with pretentious rhetoric, deliberate obscurantism, and unintelligibility. When Cambridge awarded him an honorary degree in 1992, it prompted a public protest from several of the UK's leading thinkers because of his 'attacks upon the values of reason, truth, and scholarship'.

Born of a Jewish family in Algeria, Derrida taught at the Ecole Nationale Superieure and the Sorbonne. His three 1967 publications, *Of Grammatology*, *Writing and Difference*, and *Speech and Phenomena*, set out the approach which brought both fame and notoriety. He describes as 'logocentric' the view giving primacy to spoken language, claiming that both spoken and written language limit our thought. His case is that Western philosophy has been based on dualisms, divisions into opposites, which have incorporated unacknowledged metaphysical notions. These surreptitious metaphysical ideas have imposed hierarchies and orders of subordination on Western thinking. Dualisms, such as life and death, sanity and insanity, conceal alternative and repressed meanings which careful textual analysis can expose.

The process of this detailed analysis of texts is called 'deconstruction'. Instead of seeking the meaning of a text, deconstructionism closely examines it to seek its etymological relations and its relationship to other texts from the same culture. Derrida rejects the idea that the text refers to the outside world, to an external standard of truth. 'There is nothing outside the text,' he says, meaning nothing except other texts. He denies there can be any secure basis for meaning and truth within language. Careful textual analysis of a text can reveal other possible meanings, and rather than seeking 'the truth' or the author's intent, it can identify alternative meanings.

Derrida's approach is critical; there is no grand system, only a tool for criticizing other systems. In seeking to expose and undermine the hierarchies of Western philosophy, his analysis aims to display new possibilities which thwart our desire for reliable meanings and unequivocal truths. The dualisms characteristic of Western thinking limit and simplify, whereas deconstruction can point to contingent and complex alternatives.

Derrida's habit of coining new words (such as 'différance', as opposed to 'différence'), and varying their meaning over time, brought charges of sheltering behind vagueness, even from his friend Foucault. Derrida's prime influence was on literary analysis and criticism, where the text is often treated independently of the author's intent, but in philosophy he has been charged with undermining the rationality that characterizes academic debate.

Two of America's greatest twentieth-century political philosophers taught together at Harvard for several decades. John Rawls
championed egalitarianism with his distributive theory of justice,
but Robert Nozick was hailed by libertarians for his entitlement
derivation of justice.

Nozick's *Anarchy, State and Utopia* (1974) was published as a
counter to Rawls' *Theory of Justice* (1971), with diametrically
different views. Nozick's defence of liberty is a moral one. He
begins with two precepts. The first is Kant's principle that others
should be treated as ends in themselves, not serving anyone
else's ends. The second is that human beings own themselves
and are not anyone else's property. This self-ownership includes
their bodies, talents, abilities, and their labour. Nozick draws the
rights which follow from these precepts. They are the rights of
ownership – to decide how these things should be used or dis-
posed of. These rights set limits on how people may treat other
people.

No one has the right to take by force the product of another's
labour. This includes redistributive taxation, taking from some to
give to others. The only just state is what Nozick calls a 'night
watchman' state. He says that only a minimal state, 'limited to
the narrow functions of protection against force, theft, fraud,
enforcement of contracts, and so on, is justified; that any more
extensive state will violate persons' rights'.

This is not anarchy, however, for without a state, people
would band together to protect their rights, and some would
specialize in doing so. From this Nozick suggests that processes
for peaceful dispute resolution would emerge, complete with
arbitrators, laws and courts, and that a minimal state guaran-
teeing justice and defence would emerge from an anarchic one.

While there are echoes of social contract theory, the

important difference is that for Nozick people's rights do not derive from such contracts, they precede them.

One of Nozick's key insights is that wealth is not there to be handed out in a 'fair' manner; it has to be *made*. If it is acquired and transferred justly, the resulting distribution must also be just. All non-entitlement theories of justice, says Nozick, must be false. In a just society, equal distribution would soon become unequal as character and talents proved their worth in voluntary transactions. 'Liberty upsets patterns; patterns destroy liberty,' he writes. Far from being narrow and restrictive, he says, the minimal state is 'inspiring' and a 'framework for utopia' because it allows people to achieve different goals.

A-Z of Entries